WEST KENT
PLACE NAMES

The Homes of Kentish Men and Maids

Anthony Poulton-Smith

WEST KENT
PLACE NAMES

The Homes of Kentish Men and Maids

CONTENTS

INTRODUCTION

For years the history of England was based on the Roman occupation. In recent years we have come to realise the influence of the Empire did not completely rewrite British history, indeed there was already a thriving culture in England well before the birth of Christ. When the Romans left our shores in the fifth century the arrival of the Anglo-Saxons was thought to herald a time of turmoil, yet they brought the culture and language which forms the basis of modern England. Later the arrival of the Norsemen saw their influence and the same is true of our place names, the vast majority of settlement names in Kent are derived from the Saxon/Old English or Old Scandinavian tongues. There are also the topographical features such as rivers and hills which still have names given to them by the Celts of the pre-Roman era.

Ostensibly place names are simply descriptions of the location, or of the uses and the people who lived there. In the pages that follow an examination of the origins and meanings of the names in Kent will reveal all. Not only will we see Saxon and Scandinavian settlements, but Celtic rivers and hills, Roman roads and even Norman French landlords who have all contributed to the evolution to some degree to the names we are otherwise so familiar with.

Not only are the basic names discussed but also districts, hills, streams, fields, roads, lanes, streets and public houses. Road and street names are normally of more recent derivation, named after those who played a significant role in the development of a town or revealing what existed in the village before the developers moved in. The benefactors who provided housing and employment in the eighteenth and nineteenth centuries are often forgotten, yet their names live on in the name found on the sign at the end of the street and often have a story to tell. Pub names are almost a language of their own. Again they are not named arbitrarily but are based on the history of the place and can open a new window on the history of our towns and villages.

Defining place names of all varieties can give an insight into history, which would otherwise be ignored or even lost. In the ensuing pages we shall examine 2,000 plus years of West Kent history. While driving around this area the author was delighted by the unique place names found in this part of the county and so, having already taken a look at, among others, *East Sussex Place Names* and *West Sussex Place Names,* turned here to Kent in the form of *West Kent Place Names* and *East Kent Place Names.* This book is the result of the author's long interest in place names which has developed over many years and is the latest in a series which continues to intrigue and surprise.

To all who helped in my research, from the librarians who produced the written word to those who pointed a lost traveller in the right direction, a big thank you.

CHAPTER ONE – A

Addington

Listed as Eddintune in 1086, the Domesday record shows this name comes from Old English *ing tun* with a Saxon or Jute personal name to tell of 'the farmstead associated with a man called Eadda or Aeddi'.

East Street is still to the east of the parish, while East Street North is found north of the M2 motorway. Woodgate is seen as Wudegate in 1232 and as Wodegate in 1270, this comes from Old English *wudu geat* and speaks of 'the way or gate to the woodland'.

It is easy to see the link between the church and the name of the Angel Inn, most likely through ownership of the land. Addington's religious links pre-date the Christian era as seen by the two barrows: the Addington Barrow has no lasted so well as the Chestnut Barrow, although both have produced finds which are now held in Maidstone Museum.

Allhallows

A name which can still be seen to be from the local twelfth century church of All Saints. The name appears in a document of 1285 as Ho All Hallows, the now lost first element from Old English *hoh* or 'spur of land'.

Avery Farm is first seen in a document from 686, the name appearing as Heabureahg. This features a Saxon or Jute personal name and Old English *eg* and telling of 'the dry land in marsh (literally 'island') of a woman called Heaburh'. This is thought to have been a true island until as recently as the ninth century. Nothing is known about this woman, although perhaps we can deduce some information. It is fairly certain Heaburh was an abbess, as there is a seventh century record of the place being granted to her by King Caedwalla as part of the lands of the monks of Medehamstede. This monastery was not in Kent or even close by, it is an old name for the city of Peterborough.

Binney Farm is seen in a document of 1291 as Bynne, this telling us it was 'within a river', not a river island (correctly an ayot) but raised ground at one bank where the land behind is lower and thus tends to be marshy. Dagnam Farm is seen as Dekeham in 1240, a name describing 'the *ham* or homestead of a man called Daeccan'. Nord Farm and Nord Corner are derived from the family of John Northe, first recorded here in 1327.

Allington

A second example of this place name, this being near Maidstone in East Kent. Recorded as Elentun in Domesday, this has a slightly different origin. Here Old English *ing tun* follows a different Saxon or Jute personal name and gives us 'the farmstead associated with a man called Aella or Aelle'.

It was only in the twentieth century this place began to grow at all. In the middle of the nineteenth century the few houses grouped around the castle brought the population to a peak of just 49 individuals. Hence many of the place names are modern creations and, it must be said, lack much imagination. For example the local industrial estate stands near the junction of the M20 and A20 roads, earning it the official name of the 20/20.

Ashurst

The earliest surviving record of this name appears in an undated document traced to around the end of the twelfth century. This record of Aeischerste points to an Old English *aesc hyrst* and 'the wooded hill of the ash trees'.

Kent welcomes us at Ashurst

Aylesford

Two early records of this name, as Aeglesforda in the tenth century and in Domesday as Ailesford. These point to a Saxon or Jute personal name and Old English *ford* and show this comes from 'the ford of a man called Aegel'.

Forstal is recorded as Fforstalle in 1348, this minor place name tells us it is found 'at the front' literally 'before the place'. It is tempting to suggest this represents somewhere on the route from London. However while it does show this was a known stop on the road, the only thing we can be certain of is the place was named by travellers from a point north of Maidstone. What is today known as Hermitage got its name as 'the land of the hermit of Longesole', Its previous name comes from *land sol* 'the long muddy pool'. From Old English *myln halh*, Millhall speaks of its location as being recognised as 'the corner of land where a mill stands'.

Kit's Coty House is seen from the seventeenth century, however the name is very much earlier and speaks of *ked coed* or 'the burial chamber in a wood'. This tomb has become eroded in recent years, exposing three upright stones and a large capstone. There is also a Little Kits Coty House, a second barrow lower down the hillside, also known as the Countless Stones.

One pub here is the Lower Bell, likely suggesting itself as it stands on Blue Bell Hill but also named to link with Upper Bell at Chatham, explained under that entry. There is also the Little Gem, a small but delightful establishment.

CHAPTER TWO – B

Bearsted

A document dating from 695 gives this name as Berghamstyde. This comes from Old English *beorg ham stede* and describes 'the homestead on a hill'.

Local names include Madginford. With records dating from as early as 832, where it appears as Megeldeuurthe, the name originated as 'the enclosure of a man called Maeghild'. Clearly the modern form has seen a change of the suffix from *worth* to *ford*, for some reason a fairly common occurrence and here showing its close proximity to the river. Milgate has been seen since the early thirteenth century, although the *miln geat* or 'way to the mill' will have existed long before this. The mill stream being fed by the Lilt, a tributary of the Len, and a river name which seems to be quite modern as there is no Old English explanation. A name from the sixteenth century when this was associated with a family called Ricard.

Roseacre Street is found as Rokesakere in 1258 and as Rokesacre in 1327, this describing 'the acre of land frequented by rooks' from Old English *hroces aecer*. Sutton Street has evolved to become the very common 'sutton', yet the origin here is *strut tun* or 'the farmstead of strife'. Here the reference is to disputed land, rather than a battle, with the addition showing it was near a Roman road. Weavering Street takes its name from the Jute or Saxon who lived here, this talking of the Waefringas, themselves known by a nickname describing them quite literally as 'wavering people'. Understood as meaning 'wandering', it seems this Jute tribe were known for being nomadic before they settled here.

In the Oak on the Green we find two elements utilised by landlords to advertise their pubs. Trees are a favourite as they not only make for an attractive sign but take advantage of a large and easily seen landmark to point to the location which, in this example, also leaves no doubt as to where that oak tree grows. The Kentish Yeoman would originally have referred to a farmer, later a military man and, as a pub name, likely both.

Beckenham

Records of this name include Beohha hammes gemaeru in 973 and as Bachenham in 1086. Here is a Saxon personal name and Old English *ham* and tells of 'the homestead of a man called Beohha'. There is an extra element in the late tenth century record, where *gemaeru* refers to 'the boundary'.

One Beckenham family left their surname on the map at Elmers End, seen as Aylmer and Eilmer in the thirteenth and fourteenth centuries. Kelsey Manor is from that Kelsey family, who held the manor of Beckenham during the thirteenth century. Similarly Rockhills recalls the de la Rokele family, who held this manor during the reign of Edward I.

Kent Street does not derive its name directly from the county but via the family of John de Kent and his home of Kent House in Beckenham. Cator Lane recalls the family headed by John Cator, former lord of the manor who is best remembered for Beckenham Place. Stumpshill Wood comes from Old English *stumbeles hyll* and, recorded as Stumelshull in 1226, speaks of 'the hill marked by tree stumps'. Foxgrove describes 'the grove frequented by foxes', it seems they were not welcome here.

Many pubs feature the old position of woodsman in the name, hence there is always room for an addition to avoid confusion. If that addition shows a warm welcome and a good time is on offer within, so much the better. Hence the most common addition to a trade name is that seen here in the Jolly Woodman.

Beult (River)

To pronounce this name correctly simply say it as if the 'u' had been omitted. The pronunciation is important for records do not begin until 1622 and the name is certainly older than seventeenth century. Thus this is probably from Old English *belg* literally 'belly, bag' and is suggesting the river is 'the swollen one', which locals will attest still happens quite regularly to flood the surrounding low-lying areas.

Bewl Water

Created in the 1970s, this reservoir takes the name of the River Bewl and was constructed in the Bewl Valley. Its name comes from exactly the same source as the Beult, Old English *belg* telling us this was also liable to flood and hence described as 'the swollen one'. Those who named this river could never have foreseen just how swollen their water source would one day become.

With a perimeter of some 17 miles, the river itself is never enough to keep the waters topped up to a storage capacity of 6,900 million gallons, hence water is pumped from the rivers Teise and Medway during winter months when water is normally more plentiful.

Bexley

Listings of this name are many, from 765 comes Bixle, by 814 this is Byxlea, in 1240 Bixle and Byxle, by 1314 this is Bexle and as Bexley for the first time in 1610. Here we find Old English *byxe leah* 'the woodland clearing by or among the box trees'. In comparison Bexleyheath is a very recent name and was not seen until the heathland to the south of Bexley was developed.

Brampton Place is from *brom tun* 'the farmstead where broom grows', albeit an unusual result. Bursted Wood comes from Old English *burna stede* 'the place by a stream', the name existing before it was given to the wood. Danson Farm's first appearance is in the fourteenth century, a name describing 'the *tun* or farmstead of a man called Denesige'. Upton is among the most common of place names, an indication this is among the most simple and indeed this is the case in meaning 'the higher farmstead'. Tile Kiln Lane marks the site of a former kiln for making tiles or the road leading to the kiln.

A name which dates from the Saxon individual who held the manor during the reign of Edward the Confessor, Foots Cray describes 'the place on the River Cray associated with a man called Goduine or Godwine Fot'. Picardy Street is first seen in documents from the middle of the sixteenth century, a name which clearly began as 'the spring or stream of the Pycard' family, the modern name has clearly been influenced by its namesake in France.

Wansunt appears as Wantesforte in 1270, from *funta* and a personal name and speaking of 'the spring of a man called Want'. Lessness Heath describes itself as 'the meadow headland', from Old English *laes ness* this is recorded as Lesneis in the Domesday record of 1086.

Pub names begin with the Woodman, a man whose task of tending to the local trees made him among the most important. In later years the image, usually shown as wearing clothes of green cloth, has been changed to the name of England's most popular outlaw, Robin Hood. So common is the name that some pubs seek a distinguishing element and here we find the name of his best known companion in the Robin Hood and Little John. A more recent figure gave his name to the Earl Haig. Douglas Haig was commander-in-chief of the British forces in France and Flanders during the First World War.

Several creative suggestions have been put forward as to the origin of the Three Blackbirds, yet although this sounds as if this is heraldic the real origin is much simpler. Whilst today the blackbird refers to just the one creature, historically this referred to those of the crow family such as the rook, crow, and jackdaw. It would have taken a skilled brush to clearly depict the three very similar birds. No surprises to find the Old Mill refers to a former use for the building.

England's national summer sport gave a name to the delightfully named Wrong 'Un public house. This refers to a delivery from a right hand leg spinner, which is released in such a manner that it turns the opposite way to his (or her) standard ball – ie turning to the leg-side (for a right hand batsman) rather than to the off-side. The correct term is the 'googly', although in Australia it is known as the 'bosie' after its creator, Bernard Bosanquet. If the surname sounds familiar it is probably down to his even better known son, Reginald Bosanquet was among the most popular newsreaders of his day.

The Drayman is an advertisement for the product through the image of the man whose job was to bring the beers to the pub.

Bidborough

Documented as Bitteberga at the end of the eleventh century, this features a Saxon or Jute personal name and Old English *beorg* to tell us of 'the hill or mound of a man called Bitta'.

Bidborough village sign

Locally we find Judge Wood, recalling the family of Galfridus Jud who were here in 1652. The Mount has an obvious origin, this referring to meeting place of the Loningborough Hundred. Tapners can be traced to the eighth century telling of 'the brushwood place of a man called Taeppa', the Saxon personal name suffixed by Old English *haes*.

The most obvious feature in Bidborough is the old windmill, now a private residence. While the earliest record of a windmill here dates from the eighteenth century, there is good evidence to suggest this building is the second on this site. No flour has been ground here since 1900, when two of the four sails were destroyed in the instant it was hit by lightning.

St Lawrence Church at Bidborough

Birling

Recorded as Boerlingas in 788 and as Berlinge in 1086, this name comes from a Saxon or Jute personal name and Old English *ingas*. Together these tell us of the '(place of) the family or followers of a man called Baerla'.

Leg Lane here remembers John Leg and his family, here by 1368.

Borough Green

Although the earliest record of this name dates from 1575, when it appears as Borrowe Grene and Middle English *grene* refers to the village green, the name itself is much older. Indeed because the name is older and there are no records from the pre-Norman era, it is difficult to see if this from Old English *burh* 'manor, borough' or from *beorg* 'hill, mound'.

Basted gets its name from Old English *beorg stede* or 'the place of the mound or barrow', the modern pronunciation rhymes with 'wasted'.

Boughton Monchelsea

Recorded as Boltone in 1086 and as Bocton Monchansy in 1278, this name is again from Old English *boc tun* and describes 'the farmstead held by charter' with an addition from the de Montchensie family, here by the thirteenth century.

Fairbourne is first seen as a place name in the Domesday record of 1086, this being from Old English *fearn burna* 'the stream where ferns grow'. Heronden began as a minor name describing 'the *denn* or woodland pasture of a man called Hyra'. Tilt's Farm is not a personal name but comes from *tilthe*, the Old English ancestor of the word 'tilth'. To 'till the soil' is now used to describe preparing it for planting, however for the Saxons was also used to refer to harvesting the crop at the end of the growing season.

First recorded as Lewode in 1425, Lywood House was built on an area known as 'the wood at the woodland clearing' from Old English *leah wudu*. Marl Pit has changed little since 1283, and can still be seen as referring to a pit where marl is gathered. This is a nutrient high soil which was spread on the land to act as a fertiliser. Petlands, first seen in 1504 and exactly as it appears today, comes from *pytt land* and warns this is 'the agricultural land where there are pits or hollows'. Wierton Place comes from 'the *tun* or farmstead of a man called Wighere', the name found as Wyhgherintone in 1225 and as Wygherton in 1313.

For many years the local ragstone was quarried here, this type of sandstone was taken from the Roman era until the quarry closed in 1960. Doubtless we have all seen something of the stone taken from here as it was used in the construction of Westminster Abbey and the Palace of Westminster.

Boxley

Domesday lists this name as Boseleu in 1086 and as Boxlea at the end of the eleventh century. From Old English *box leah* this describes 'the woodland clearing where box trees grow'.

Dun Street appears from the sixteenth century, describing 'the way to the hills'. Note this is not a road name but a place name, the road being known as

Dun Street Road. A document dated 1390 shows one John Farenthe in residence, the family being the origin of the local name of Farthings. Horish Wood comes from Old English *horh gewaesc* and describes 'the filthy ground washed by water'.

Osierland Wood first appears in the sixteenth century as Hosiersland and, rather than being 'the cultivated land where willow grows' appears to be manorial even though nothing survives to support this. Nearby we find the name of Tyland, seen as Tylond in 1535 and likely from *teag land* or 'the agricultural land by an enclosure'. Cowbeck Wood is not recorded before the fifteenth century, although that record of Cukebake seems less likely than the modern form which would give us 'the stream near where cows are reared'.

Boxley Abbey is a ruin but still a scheduled monument. Founded in 1143 and home to monks from Clairvaux Abbey in France, the abbot here in 1171 helped to arrange the burial of Thomas a Becket, murdered Archbishop of Canterbury. Two decades later another abbot rode across the continent searching for Richard the Lionheart and indeed found him in Bavaria.

Brasted

Listed as Briestede in Domesday and as Bradestede at the end of the eleventh century, this name comes from Old English *brad stede* and refers to 'the broad place'.

Nicholas le Chapman was associated with Chapman's Wood by 1313. Clinton Lane and Clinton Wood take their names from John de Clinton, lord of the manor of Broxham by the end of the fourteenth century. Newman's Hill can be traced back to 1313 and the family of John le Newman.

The local pub is the White Hart, a name which came to prominence in the late fourteenth century with the accession of Richard II. It only maintained its popularity through being the generic name for a pub, much as the vacuum cleaner is more often said to be 'a hoover'.

Napoleon III lived here for a time. He later became President of the First French Republic and ruler of the Second French Empire, a position he was elected to. Louis-Napoleon Bonaparte was the heir and nephew of his infamous predecessor.

Bredhurst

The earliest surviving record of this name dates from 1240, where the name appears as Bredehurst. This name comes from Old English *bred hyrst* and describes 'the wooded hill where boards are obtained', ostensibly an early lumber supplier.

Kemsley Street dates from at least the late twelfth century. This is 'the woodland clearing of a man called Cymes' with the 'street' a comparatively recent addition. Lidsing comes from *hliodesingas*, a Saxon name describing 'the noisy people' – not a derogatory term but a nickname for the local tribe. Monkdown Wood hardly needs much explanation for it does indeed show 'the down or hill of the monks' as it was held by Boxley Abbey.

While none of the gold hidden away at the Dissolution of the Monasteries has ever been found, the place name is synonymous with a famous treasure – the Bredhurst Paten. Made from copper and gilded, this held the communion bread and is now part of the religious collection held by the Victoria and Albert Museum. Found and restored in 1907, it is one of only four in existence and is priceless.

Brenchley

From a Saxon or Jute personal name and Old English *leah* this name describes 'the woodland clearing of a man called Braenci'. The name is recorded as Bruencesle around the end of the eleventh century.

Birchett Wood seems to have been brought here as a surname from a family known as atte Byrchette or 'dwellers by the birch copse'. Burr's Hill is from the family of Richard le Borre, here by 1278, although the name is also spelled le Burre in 1292, Burr in 1327, and Bur in 1347. Early records of Castle Hill show this is at the opposite end of the scale from 'castle', this being Old French *case* and describes the '(place) of the dweller in the hovel'.

Catt's Place is derived from the family of Jordan le Cat, here in 1240. Chillmill is made up of two Old English words, *celde myln* describing 'the mill by a spring' and listed as Childemelle in 1327. The Knowle is recorded as

Cnolle in 1226 and Knolle in 1327, this is from Old English *cnoll* and describes 'the hillock'. Longbrooks has been recorded since the early fourteenth century, from *lang broc* and describes 'the long marshy ground'. Old Hay, Great Hay and Little Hay share the element from *haga* or 'the hedged enclosure', with three additions which are self-explanatory.

Saxby's Hill is named from the seventeenth century, when a large family recorded both as Saxbie and Saxby were here. Records from the thirteenth century of Warbbutone and Warblintone point to an origin for Warrington Place as 'the farmstead of a woman called Waerburh'. Flightshot comes from Old English *flicce scyrte* and describes 'the shortened aea of land'. Market Heath does not show the location of a market but is a reminder of the family of John Marcote, first recorded here in 1377.

One man who has no places named after him is Wat Tyler, a man held to be born here in the early fourteenth century. Whether he was wrong or right, the leader of the Peasants Revolt is as an important a part of Kent's history as anyone and would certainly merit some recognition if we could be certain this was his place of birth.

Brenchley Oast House

Brockley

Listed as Brocele in 1182, Brocleg in 1226, Brokele in 1328, and Brookley in 1690. Here is a name from Old English *broc leah* which tells of 'the woodland clearing near marshy ground'.

Brockley was once famous for its market gardens, the place took advantage of the huge amount of so-called 'night soil' from London used as a fertiliser. This refers to the contents of the privies brought to the fields here and which contributed to Brockley's reputation for excellent rhubarb.

Bromley

A common enough English place name and one which is invariably derived from Old English *brom leah* and describes 'the woodland clearing where broom grows'. This name appears as Bromleag in 862 and as Bronlei in 1086.

To the east is Bickley, found as Byckeleye in 1279 and describing 'the *leah* or woodland clearing of a man called Bicca'. Widmore is seen as Withme in 1226, this coming from *withig mere* and describing 'the pool at the withy or willows'. Hook Farm features the element *hoc*, the Old English for 'a projection of land'. Martin's Hill came here as a family name, this a reminder of John Marton, first seen here in a document dated 1603.

Blackbrook describes 'the brook in dark marshy land'. Blackwall comes from *blaec wielle* 'the dark-coloured spring'. Mazzards Wood takes the name of the family of Roger and Thomas Mosard, recorded as living at Bromley in 1327. St Blaise's Well gave a name to St Blaize Avenue, there was once an oratory here dedicated to this saint. Turpington Farm has early records of Tropinden and Tropyndenn, this from Old English *denn* and a Saxon personal name and telling of 'woodland pasture of a man called Troppa'.

The Crown public house has a name which is among the most common in the land, this clearly showing a link to the monarchy but ostensibly a patriotic establishment. At the Bird in Hand the message is that heard in the adage which continues "...is worth two in the bush" telling customers to be content with what is on offer as wishing for the unattainable is pointless

In the Star and Garter the image refers to the highest order of chivalry, the Most Noble Order of the Garter. While it was certainly instituted by Edward II in the middle of the fourteenth century, the story told of its origins seems to have developed much later. It is said a court ball was in full swing when a garter slipped from the leg of the Countess of Salisbury, universally acclaimed the fairest lady in the land. To save the poor woman's blushes the king picked it up and slid it onto his own leg saying *"Honi soit qui mal y pense"* or "Evil be to him who evil thinks" and then quite coincidentally became the motto of the order.

The Tigers Head is taken directly from the coat of arms of Sir Francis Walsingham. Although he became principal secretary to Queen Elizabeth I, this local man is more often known as the 'spymaster' as a result of his leading role in revealing a Catholic plot to oust the queen and replace her with Mary, Queen of Scots. Earl Amherst was Governor-General of India from the early nineteenth century. William Amherst also held the title of Viscount Holmesdale, which linked him to the county of Kent. His name is seen outside the Lord Holmesdale public house, although the road here is spelled wrongly as Homesdale Road.

Henry Paget, 1st Marquis of Anglesey is remembered for his military career, he led the infamous Charge of the Light Brigade in the Crimean War, and later a political career. His title shares the spelling with the Welsh island, however the pub is given as the Anglesea Arms. Paget would certainly have met the Queen and her eldest daughter, Princess Victoria Adelaide. No pub named after her but the Prince Frederick commemorates her husband, Frederick William, Crown Prince of Prussia.

The Royal Bell Hotel is another name showing royal connections, although this establishment off Market Square closed some years ago. It does live on in literature, however, the name is mentioned in Jane Austen's *Pride and Prejudice.*

Brookland

As with the previous name this is quite easily seen as 'the cultivated land by a brook'. The name is recorded as Broklande in 1262 and comes from Old English *broc land*.

Rather more interesting is the local stories behind the unique church which has a spire made entirely of wood which stands quite separately from the main body of the church. Traditionally this was the result of the steeple looking down upon a marriage ceremony and seeing the most beautiful bride tying the knot with a quite ugly groom, whereupon the steeple jumped off the church. A cheekier story suggests the steeple fell from the church in a faint when seeing a wedding where the bride was a virgin. The real reason is the weight of the two could not be supported on what was once marshland.

Broomfield

Listings of this name include Brunfelle in Domesday and as Brumfeld around the end of the eleventh century. This is derived from Old English *brom feld* and describes 'the open land where broom grows'.

Recorded as Cyninges firhthe in 850, this is easy to see as 'the woodland of the king' and seen as the name of King's Wood on modern maps. The local is the Huntsman and Horn, both showing the premises were associated with the hunt, possibly as a meeting place or even as a former occupation of the landlord.

CHAPTER THREE – C

Catford

The earliest surviving record of this document comes from 1254 where it appears exactly as the modern form. Here Old English *catt ford* describes 'the ford frequented by wild cats'.

A modern place name is found in a region developed to provide emergency housing following the end of the Second World War. Some 188 prefabricated bungalows were erected in what was known as the Excalibur Estate, although why it was named was never recorded.

Chainhurst

A name first seen in 1278, where the name is recorded as Cheyney, de Cheneye, and de Cheuenye. All these have led to the eventual form of Cheyney's, then Chayners, and eventually the modern Chainhurst.

As with much of the county, known as the Garden of England, fruit and vegetables were produced with hops the most important crop.

Chalk

Records of this name include Cealca in the tenth century and as Celca in Domesday. Derived from Old English *cealc* this does indeed mean what it says today, although it should be understood as '(place at) the chalk'.

Filborough Farm can be traced back to a late thirteenth century minor place name from Old English *fealu beorg* and describing 'the mound near the fallow land'. A Roman villa was discovered here in 1961, although Chalk is better known for its link to the writing of Charles Dickens. His time here with his new bride, Catherine Hogarth, is reflected in the first few chapters of *Pickwick Papers*, which was first published as a serial, while the village forge appears as the home and workplace of Joe Gargery in *Great Expectations*.

Charlton

A common English place name and one which always refers to 'the farmstead of the freemen or peasants'. Derived from Old English *ceorl tun*, this name appears as Cerletone in 1086.

The church is the final resting place of Spencer Perceval (1762–1812). For a politician to be remembered for his death instead of his life would probably not have been appreciated by the former prime minister. He was known to have drunk very much less than most MPs, vociferously opposed the slave trade, hunting, gambling and adultery, gave regularly and generously to charity, and wrote extensively of the time he enjoyed with his twelve children. He was unlucky enough to have several major crises to deal with during his term of office, problems largely beyond his control. However he seemed to have successfully negotiated the tempestuous waters until meeting John Bellingham, a merchant with a grievance, on the evening of 11 May. Bellingham shot him in the chest at close range in the lobby of the House of Commons, making Spencer Perceval the answer to the common pub quiz question of "Who was the first, and so far only, prime minister of Britain to be assassinated?"

Chart Sutton

As with the previous two entries, this name features the Old English element *cert* or 'rough ground' and the earliest records are as Caert in 814 and as Certh in 1086. There is a later record from 1280 as Chert juxta Suthon, telling us the addition is from its location near Sutton Valence.

Rabbit's Cross recalls the family of Thomas Rabbet, here by 1613, with an addition referring to a marker. Lamb's Cross was named from the family represented by William Lambe, himself recorded in a document from 1470.

Chatham

Found as Cetham in 880 and as Ceteham in 1086, this name comes from Celtic *ced* and Old English *ham* and speaks of 'the homestead by the wood'.

The local name of Dan's Hill is from a former resident, Arnold in the Dane was here in 1313, his name meaning 'dweller in the valley'. Shawstead Road features an old minor place name, first seen in the thirteenth century this is derived from *sceard stede* and tells of 'the place where shards of pottery have been discovered'. Lower Ensden and Upper Ensinge are related, they share a common ancestry, The latter describes the '(place) of the family or followers of a man called Esne', while the former speaks of 'the woodland pasture of the (place of the) family or followers of a man called Esne'.

Horsted is traditionally held to be named from it being the burial place of the famous Jute leader Horsa. More likely this is from Old English *hors stede* and literally speaking of 'the place of the horses', with the name recorded as Horstede in the late seventh century.

The pub known as the Upper Bell was named as it was at one end of a road only wide enough for one stagecoach to pass, the bell rang to warn such was on its way and to await its passing before entering this section of road. Today being in charge of the management of woodland through planting and coppicing is an important position, however not as important as the days when it provided fuel and building materials and thus the origin of the Woodsman public house.

Chatham's links to the sea make the Shipwrights Arms almost obligatory, the Worshipful Company of Shipwrights the largest of the livery companies. In the White Lion is a strong image found in many coats of arms and representing such leading lights as Edward IV, the earls of March, and the dukes of Norfolk. Count Karl August von Alten, commanded the German Legion allied to the British in both the Peninsular Wars and at Waterloo and, more importantly for Chatham drinkers, gave his name to the Von Alten public house.

The General At Sea does not refer to a specific individual but to any of several former army leaders who have later headed forces on the ocean. To some degree this is similar to the Medway Queen, not a reference to a monarch but the name of a boat. In the Boatswain and Call we see a reference to the piping aboard of a senior officer or important visitor to a vessel. The Hen and Chickens is taken from the terms for different sizes of drinking vessel, thus advertising the product.

The Trafalgar Maid is the rebuilt pub which stands next to the home of Jane Townshend. She earned her nickname by being aboard *HMS Euryalus* at the Battle of Trafalgar. The pub was built on the rubble after the earlier pub was bombed during the Second World War. Ironically the earlier pub was known as the New Inn. At the Ordinary Man we find a name taken from what was said to the Archbishop of Canterbury as he travelled through the streets thronged by well-wishers. Yet "I'm just an ordinary man" would not have been how the cheering crowds saw King George V on the occasion of his Silver Jubilee.

Chattenden

With the earliest record dating from around the end of the eleventh century as Chatendune, this name comes from a Saxon or Jute personal name and Old English *dun* and tells of 'the hill of a man called Ceatta'.

The local name of Haven Street was, until comparatively recently for a place name, known as Haydon Street. This original name came from *haeth dun* 'the hill growing with heather', the present name appears from the seventeenth century and must have been a deliberate attempt to make the place more appealing. Lillechurch is from 'the *cirice* or church of a woman called Lillan'.

Chelsfield

Domesday records this name as Cillesfelle in 1086. Here is an Old English place name and one with two possible meanings. Either the first element is a personal name with the suffix *feld* and describes 'the open land of a man called Ceorl' or *ceorl feld* and 'the open land of the freemen or peasants'.

Cacket's Farm is a corruption of Old English *cald cot* or 'the cold or exposed cottages'. This is a rather different modern form of a common English name which would normally be seen as Calcot or Caldecot. Hewitts comes from Old English *hiewet* meaning 'the place of the cleared woodland'.

Pub names include the Bo-Peep Inn, known as such from the middle of the eighteenth century, prior to which it was the White Hart. The name is linked to the smuggling of wool and held to be where such was brought by smugglers through a cave system linked to a nearby well.

Chevening

A name from Celtic *cevn* and Old English *ingas* which probably means the '(place of) the dwellers by the ridge'. The name is recorded as Chivening in 1199.

Brockhill Wood is derived from Old English *broc halh* and speaks of 'the hill near marshy ground'. Hyde's Forest remembers the name of the family who held this land and lived at neighbouring Sundridge in the seventeenth and eighteenth centuries. Star Hill can be found as far back as 1313, when a document recalls the family of Richard and Paget le Ster. A *scaga* or 'shaw' is a 'copse' and, in the case of Edward Shaw, was named from the family of John and Jordan Edward, here in 1338.

Chiddingstone

Listed as Cidingstane in an undated document from around the early twelfth century, this name probably comes from Old English *ing stan* with a Saxon or Jute personal name and telling us this was 'the stone associated with a man called Cidd or Cidda'. Chiddingstone Causeway marks the location of a very old route. Chiddingstone Hoath takes the name of Chiddingstone and adds Old English *haeth* 'the heathland', which has been corrupted to Hoath. Nearby Chiddinghurst shares the origin, this being 'the wooded hill associated with the people of a man called Cidd or Cidda'.

The stone in question is very visible on the outskirts of the village. It has always been held to have been a meeting place, some hold this was a meeting place for Druids, although there is no evidence to show the place was associated with the Celts. Later stories suggest it was where nagging wives were put on display, again quite fictional, when this is simply a natural feature used as a boundary marker.

St Luke's Church at Chiddingstone Causeway

Batfold Wood is from *beorc falod* or 'the pen or fold near a birch tree' and is found as Berkefaud in 1240. Breeches Wood takes the name of the De La Breche family, recorded here in 1270. The name of Moorden comes from Old English *mor denn*, telling of 'the moorland pasture'. From Old English *ceap stede* and recorded as Chepsted in 1240, Chested speaks of 'the market place'. Frienden speaks of 'the woodland pasture of a man called Helfrith', and is recorded as Helfrethingdenn in 814 and as Frendenne by 1239. Stonelake comes from *stan lacu* and describes 'the stony stream'.

Gasson's Wood takes the name of the family of William Gasson, who came here from Hever before 1648. The name of Gilwyns shows this was associated with the family of John and Richard Gylewin during the thirteenth century. Hale is found around the country, and at least eleven other places in Kent alone, almost always from *halh* and describing 'the nook of land'. Somerden Green is only a minor place today, this from *sumor denn* or 'the woodland pasture used in summer', but was once more important as the meeting place of the Somerden Hundred.

Tyehurst is found from the thirteenth century, a name derived from Old English *teag hyrst* and describing 'the wooded hill near an enclosure'. Vexour has records of Hexore in 1278, Ffexore in 1338, and as Fexore in 1382, representing Old English *feax ora* or 'the coarse or rough grass growing on the bank'. William Pigott is documented as the head of the family living here in 1567, the name remembered by the modern name of Picketts. During the fourteenth century the Peltebem family were living in the area now known as Pilbeams and named from them.

Chipstead

Even without the record as Chepsteda in 1191 it would be quite easy to see this as coming from Old English *ceap stede* and telling us it was 'the market place'.

Dryhill is a local name which does not mean quite what it seems for it would be impossible to believe the rainfall was appreciably lower than anywhere near. Here it is simply drier as the raised land would drain while the surrounding area was principally marshy.

Chislehurst

Recorded as Cysellhyrst in 973, this is easily to see as coming from Old English *cisel hyrst* and referring to 'the gravelly wooded hill'. Chislehurst Caves were where chalk and flint were mined, used as an air raid shelter during the Second World War, and became the venue for rock concerts given by Jimi Hendrix, The Who, and The Rolling Stones.

Minor names include Frognal, a name which seem to mean 'the corner of land where frogs are found'. However this is a comparatively modern name, one likely influenced by its namesake near Teynham. Previously this place was known as Frogpool, from *frogga pol* or 'the pool known for its frogs'. Records of the name which is today seen as Kemnal Manor have been found back to the thirteenth century, this speaking of 'the *hol* or hollow of a man called Cyma'.

Both Great Thrift and Little Thrift come from Old English *ffrythe* and telling of 'the woodland'. Holbrook, dating from at least the thirteenth century as Hallerebrok, this from Old English *haelor broc* and speaking of 'the marshy place in a hollow'. From *feld* and a Saxon personal name comes the modern Radfield, listed since the thirteenth century and telling us this was 'the open land of a man called Hroda'.

The Imperial Arms is a pub named for the town being home to Napoleon III from around 1870. He was nephew and heir to his more famous namesake. A soldier in the Gordon Highlanders appears outside the Gordon Arms, probably showing an association between that regiment and a former landlord.

Cliffe

Listed as Cliua in the tenth century and as Clive in Domesday, this comes from Old English *clif* and refers to the '(place at) the cliff or bank'.

Both Allen's Hill and Allen's Pond share an origin of the family of John Aleyn, recorded here in 1327. Cardens Wood and Cardens Farm is derived from a family seen here throughout the thirteenth and fourteenth centuries as Cardon, Kardon and Cardoun. Mortimers is derived from a family name, documented evidence of one Hugh de Mortimer in the thirteenth century tells us he was a rector of the parish.

Rye Street comes from Old English *ryge feld* or 'the open land where rye is grown'. For reasons unknown the original *feld*, which would be expected to become – field, was changed to Street. Well Penn Road takes the name of a minor name, seen in a fifteenth century document and coming from *wielle pund* or 'the pound near a spring'.

One man who might merit a street named after him in the future is Henry Pye. He brought a number of modern farming practices to Kent, including the use of steam engines built at Rochester for ploughing and threshing. However it was his actions in draining the marshland and drastically reducing the number of cases of malaria which earned him the soubriquet King of the Hundreds.

Cobham

Records of this place name include Cobba hammes mearce in 939 and as Cobbeham in 1197. Here the Saxon or Jute personal name follows Old English *ham* and speaks of 'the homestead of a man called Cobba'. Note the earliest form also features Old English *mearc* or 'boundary'.

Ashenbank Wood is recorded as simply Ashen Bank in 1698, when the place was known for 'the ash trees at the bank of land'. Battle Street takes the name of Battle in Sussex, the actual site of the Battle of Hastings, and brought here as a surname with Robert Batayll the first individual recorded here in 1270. Burleigh is from Old English *bur leah* 'the clearing with a bower'.

Chambers Hill Wood derives its name from the former landowner, here before 1572. Claylane Wood took its name from the way which passed by here, itself from Old English *aet thaere claeigan lane* or 'at the clayey lane', a warning this route had a tendency to be muddy and sticky making passage difficult. From Old English *col wudu* and recorded as Colewood since the end of the seventeenth century, Cole Wood is a reminder of 'a place where charcoal was burned'.

Henhurst is recorded from the tenth century, it comes from Old English *henn hyrst* and speaks of 'the wooded hill frequented by hen birds'. Note these are not hens but simply female birds. Jeskins Court recalls the fourteenth century when John Josekyn is the first of the family recorded here. The farm of 360 acres which later bore this name has become a vast area controlled by the Forestry Commission. A name seen as Knight's Place today is a reminder this was associated with the Knights Templars. Round Street is not seen until 1630, undoubtedly coming from the name of a family although no records of such survive.

Seen as Skarelettes in 1572, Scalers Hill must be manorial, although no record of the family survives. Sole Street comes from *sol straet* or 'the muddy pool at or near the Roman road'. With William's Hill an old family, here between 1558 and 1625, have left their mark, although these old documents give their surname as Willmans. In Winstead Hill we find a name describing 'the windy place'. Winterham Hill is seen as Wyntrame in 1572, this coming from Old English *winter hamm* and telling of 'the hemmed in land where livestock are pastured during winter months'.

Cobham Hall was home to the Blythe family who hailed from Cornwall. Having made their name in the capital, later generations came to Cobham as earls of Darnley and are remembered by the Darnley Arms public house.

Cooling

Records of this name include Culingas in 808 and as Colinges in 1086. This comes from a Saxon or Jute personal name and Old English *ingas*, together they tell of the '(settlement of) the family or followers of a man called Cul or Cula'.

Broomy Farm is clearly 'the place where broom grows'. Eastborough is another simple name to define, here *east burh* sees the suffix used in the later manorial sense to describe 'the eastern manor'.

Cooling Castle was home to Sir John Oldcastle, at least it became so following his marriage to the heiress of Cobham and allowing him to enter parliament as Lord Cobham. Oldcastle's association with Kent was short lived for within eight years he was dead. Convicted of heresy this man, often styled the King of Lollards, had been hanged, his body and the gallows were burned so quickly after the noose tightened it was never clear whether Sir John was still alive or not. Shakespeare's Falstaff is very much based on Sir John Oldcastle.

Cowden

Listed as Cudenna at the end of the eleventh century, this comes from Old English *cu denn* and describes 'the pasture for cows'.

Blowers Hill takes the name of the family of le Blowere, recorded here in 1278. Cole Allen must also come from a surname, no records have been found but would have something akin to Allen or perhaps Alleyn, with the first element telling us it was in a comparatively exposed position. From Old English *denn* following a Saxon or Jute personal name, Crippenden describes 'the woodland pasture of a man called Cryppa and is recorded as Cryppenden in 1278.

Ludwells has been known since at least the early fourteenth century, a name describing the *hlaw* or 'hill of a man called Luda'. Waystrode Farm is seen as Weystrode in 1292, the name from Old English *hwaeg strod* or 'the 'the sour marshland overgrown with brushwood'. Leighton Manor is a modern corruption of Lecton, as it was recorded in 1260, shows this is from *leac tun* and describes 'the vegetable garden'. Note the Old English *leac* has become the modern 'leek' but was once used as the generic term for all vegetables and indeed due to the leek being the ubiquitous ingredient in every Saxon recipe.

Coxheath

Documented as Cokkyshoth in 1489 and as Coxhoth in 1585, this tells of 'the heathland belonging to the Cok family. One Gilbert Cok is documented as being here in 1339.

One minor name was simple enough to define from the 1278 record of Valeye, yet today it leaves no room for doubt as The Valley. In 1967 Coxheath became home to the World Custard Pie Throwing Championships, attracting upwards of eighty competitors from as far afield as Japan, Canada, Finland and Germany. At first only men were allowed to compete as the stronger male would undoubtedly have an unfair advantage. However soon it was thrown open to all and thereafter nearly every winner was female.

Cray (Foots, North, St Mary, & St Pauls)

Here the basic place name comes from the river, the River Cray is a Celtic name describing 'the fresh or clean one'. Records of these places are plentiful, seen as Craegan in the tenth century, as Craie in Domesday, as Fotescraei and Northcraei in the eleventh century, and as Creye sancte Marie in 1257 and Creyoaulin in 1291. Here the additions refer, in order, to possession by a man named Fot at the time of Domesday, to the most northerly of the settlements, and to the dedications of the respective churches to St Mary and to St Paulinus.

Cookham Farm began as a settlement in its own right, 'the homestead of the cooks'. Crockley Green is recorded as the Crockhill in 1441 and Crockey Green in 1559, this being Old English *crocc eg* 'the enclosure where pots are made'. Gattons is a minor name from *gat tun* and recorded as Gatton in 1301 when it was known as 'the farmstead where goats are reared'.

Hoblingwell Wood, the name also seen in the earlier Hobdodlane, show hobdod as the early form of the modern 'hobgoblin'. We also find an alternative name of Powkelane in 1424, this having the same meaning as Old English *puca* means 'demon'. Clearly this part of St Paul's Cray was considered the haunt of these mischevious creatures.

Public houses begin with the Wanderer, an invitation to partake of refreshment for the traveller. In the Crayfish the pub name was clearly influenced by the place name.

Crayford

Listed as Creiford in 1199 and coming from 'the ford over the River Cray', as with the previous entry the river name describes 'the fresh or clean one'.

Barnes Cray is a reminder of the Barne family, eighteenth century landowners whose name preceded that of the river. Elmhurst is seen as Elmehurst in 1327 and Elmherst in 1348, coming from *elm hyrst* and describes 'the wooded hill of elms'. May Place is recorded as May Street in 1748 and seems certain to be a contraction of St Mary.

Many streets and squares are named after Queen Charlotte, consort of George III, but surprisingly few pubs. In the Royal Charlotte we have a different and possibly unique reference to the lady who was popular on the Continent, not only as a person but as a patron of the arts. At the Bear and Ragged Staff we see an heraldic image today used to represent Warwickshire, but here for the Neville family, Earls of Warwick.

The ford which gave Crayford its name stands almost adjacent to the river's confluence with the Darent. Clearly this was a natural barrier and would have been seen as an ideal defensive point. The Anglo-Saxon Chronicle was written some four centuries later but does state this was the site of the bloodiest of battles where Hengist and Aesc defeated the Britons and the kingdom of Kent was founded.

Crofton

The earliest known record comes from the eighth century as Croptun. Here the Old English elements *cropp tun* combine to tell of 'the farmstead by a hill'.

Culverstone Green

The earliest surviving record comes from 1381 as Culversole. With the addition of Middle English *grene*, this name comes from comes from Old English *culfre sol* 'the miry or muddy place frequented by doves'.

To the east is Harvel, a hamlet recorded in a document dated 939 as Heorot felda. This tenth century record is almost perfect Old English, where *heorot feld* describes 'the open land where harts or stags are seen'. Hodsoll Street comes from a personal name and *hol* telling of 'the hollow of a man called Hod'. Dowde's Church recalls the late tenth century landholder Dud, whose name is also seen in the lost place name of Dudeslande.

Cuxton

Documented as Cucolanstan in 880 and as Coclestane in 1086, this comes from a Saxon or Jute personal name and Old English *stan* and speaks of 'the boundary stone of a man called Cucola'.

Upper Bush and Lower Bush share an origin recorded as Beresse in 1147 and as Berherssc in 1243, this coming from *bere ersc* 'the field of barley stubble'. Today such stubble would be ploughed back into the soil fairly soon after harvesting. Even centuries ago the stubble would only have been here for six months of the year. Place names describe a specific place and, as stubble would be common to every piece of land where crops were grown, we can deduce, for reasons unknown, it seems the crop was harvested and stubble left for some time. Longhoes Wood comes from *lang hoh* and tells of 'the long spur of land'.

Archaeologists have traced the history of this area back around 200,000 years and the first evidence of human activity. In 1962 a remarkable cache of 196 hand axes was discovered, these now on display in the British Museum. Moving forward to the first century AD the Romans were here, a villa has been discovered beneath the present-day churchyard. This church was founded by the Saxons and also shows a great deal of Norman architecture. Oddly the church was built aligned north-east to south-west, a mistake recalled by the lines: "He that would see a church miswent, let him go to Cucklestane in Kent."

CHAPTER FOUR – D

Darenth

This is a name found as Daerintan in the tenth century and as Tarent in Domesday. This is a river name, the River Darent is of Celtic origins meaning 'where the oak trees grow'. One small tributary of the Darent is the Cranford, where the river name has taken a place name describing 'the river crossing frequented by cranes'.

Betsham, correctly pronounced as if the 'h' were missing, is from *ham* and a Saxon personal name and tells of 'the homestead of a man called Baeddi'. Green Street Green speaks of itself as 'the Roman road overgrown by grass', the original *grene straet* added to by Middle English *grene*. Jacob's Lane recalls 1480, when the family of Stephen Jacobe were living here.

The Colyer family were living here by the end of the eighteenth century in the form of farmer John Colyer. They are recalled by the naming of the Colyer Arms.

Dartford

Listed in Domesday as Tarentefort, this place name speaks of 'the place at the fort over the River Darent'. As stated previously the Darent is a Celtic river name meaning 'where oak trees grow'.

The Brent has evolved from Old English *bremthe* telling of 'the land overgrown with broom'. Bugden Farm is first recorded in the fourteenth century as Bulkeden, probably from *bulluc denn* and describes 'the pasture where bullocks are raised'. Bullace Lane appears as Baletts Lane in 1471 and as Bulletts Lane in 1535, this being varying spelling of the name of the landowner. Howbury Lane is recorded as Littelho in 1226, this describing 'the little spur of land'. Joyce Green Lane recalls 1334 and the family of Richard Joce, while Marsh Street is self-explanatory. Listed as Longereche in the fourteenth century, *lang raec* Longreach refers to 'the long ridge;'.

Pub names begin with the Cressy Arms. This family were certainly in Dartford at the end of the eighteenth century, for that was when the future Professor Edward Cressy was born. He grew up to become a noted architect and civil engineer, a profession also taken up by his son Edward Jnr. A name found since the early ninth century, and one common to all parts of England, Maplehurst is from Old English *mapuldor hyrst* or 'the wooded hill with maple trees'.

Overy Street points to its location 'over the river' from Old English *ofer ea* and first recorded in 1315. From Old English *pyttes feld* or 'the open land with pits or hollows' comes Pitfield, a name recorded as Pettesfeld, Pettefelde, and Pettesfeld from the thirteenth century. Southfield House was built exactly where it says it was, on 'the southern open land'. Stanham Farm appears exactly as the modern form as early as 1270, the name from *stan hamm* or 'the water meadow by stony ground'. Fulwich Lane is recorded as Foleswyk in 1270, a name from Old English *fugoles wic* and speaking of 'the farm where birds or fowl are kept'.

Any pub named the Phoenix shows a rebirth, occasionally of the pub itself but also used, and for the same reason, in a coat of arms such as that of the Seymour family, dukes of Somerset. The Hufflers Arms is quite different, for here is a name referring to those who ferried supplies to ships anchored offshore, despite having no legal permission to do so. Note the 'arms' takes advantage of the modern idea of it being instantly recognised as a pub name.

The Tollgate Inn is a reminder that once travellers were required to pay to use a road. For pubs to occupy these points was quite natural. The Wat Tyler was named after the man who led the Peasant's Revolt in 1381 and killed for his part in it. At the Oddfellows we find a pub advertising itself as a meeting place for the Independent Order of Oddfellows, a friendly society operating throughout the United Kingdom and in several other countries around the world.

Today the name of the place is synonymous with the Dartford Tunnel. While a part of the M25 orbital it is officially the A282, allowing non-motorway traffic to use the tunnel of almost a mile in length or to cross the bridge span of 500 yards.

Deptford

Seen as Depeforde in 1293, this is from Old English *deop ford* and warns travellers who would cross here that this was 'a deep ford'.

Historically this place name is associated with its docks, although little remains today. Among the pages of history written in Deptford are the knighting of Sir Francis Drake by Elizabeth I, the departure point for Captain Cook's third voyage in command of the *Resolution*, and the murder of playwright Christopher Marlowe.

Detling

Recorded as Detlinges in the eleventh century, this name features a Saxon or Jute personal name and Old English *ingas* and tells us it was the '(place of) the family or followers of a man called Dyttel'.

Broader Lane is not what it seems, the lane took the name of the place known as *brad ora* 'the broad bank'. Pollyfield Farm is recorded in a document dated 1240 as Polehull, from *pol hyll* this is 'the hill over the pools' with the suffix –field a comparatively modern change. At the Cock Horse Inn we find a reminder of this establishment being where horses were stabled to help pull heavy loads up the steep hill before returning awaiting the next load.

Downe

Recorded as Doune in 1316, this is from Old English *dun* and is understood to refer to the '(place at) the hill'.

Farthing Street gets its name from the 'fourth part (of land)', a name recorded as Ferthyng in a document dated 1366. Snotsdale Wood can be traced to Snettesdele in 1297, this from Old English *dael* and a Saxon personal name telling of 'the valley of a man called Snot'.

Dunton Green

First seen in a document from 1244 as Dunington, this name comes from a Saxon or Jute personal name and Old English *ing tun* and refers to 'the farmstead associated with a man called Dunn or Dunna'.

Rye House is a local name for a house standing on land which is dry when compared to the land around and this is the origin of the name. The place gets its name from Middle English *atter eye*, one of many examples of the final letter of the first word migrating to the beginning of the next when it ends in a vowel, to tell of this place as literally 'at the island'.

CHAPTER FIVE – E

Eccles

A name derived from Celtic *egles*, a word specifically describing 'a Romano-British Christian church'. The name is recorded as Aecclesse around 975 and as Aiglessa in 1086.

Eden (River)

Many suggestions for the origin of this name, including a fanciful idea this is related to the Biblical garden of the same name. Thankfully this is now universally seen as an example of back-formation, named from the town of Edenbridge discussed under its own entry. Of course the river was here well before the Saxon settlement, when it cannot have been known by its present name as the name of Edenbridge could not exist before these people arrived in the fifth century AD. No speculation as to the earlier name can be made without further information.

Edenbridge

The earliest known record of this name dates from the end of the eleventh century where it appears as Eadelmesbregge. Here is a Saxon or Jute personal name and Old English *brycg*, together referring to 'the bridge of a man called Eadhelm'.

Batchelor's Wood is first seen in 1566 as Bachelers, which can only be a reminder of an unrecorded local owner. Bough Beech Reservoir covers the area which would once have been marked by 'the bowed beech tree', a marker described by Old English *bogen bece*. Broxham Manor is from *ham* or 'homestead of a man called Brocc'. Originally Mowshurst appears to have been 'the wood on the hill marked by moss', from Old English *meos hyrst*. Crouch

House Green comes from Middle English *crouche hus* or 'the house near a cross'.

Plenty of castles in the county as shown by this fingerpost at Bough Beech

Clatfields is recorded as Gleappenfelda in 973, an Old English name describing 'the open land of a man called Glaeppa' where *feld* follows the Saxon or Jute personal name. Listed as Cobbingeby in 1232 and Cobbyngebure in 1316, this being 'the *burh* belonging to Cobham', here *burh* used in the later sense of 'manor' rather than the earlier 'fortified place'. Medhurst Row has remained unchanged since the end of the twelfth century, this coming from Old English *maed hyrst* and telling of 'the wooded hill above the meadow'.

A splendid village sign and fingerpost at Four Elms

Four Elms is a recent name, created for a new development and also used for the local pub. Gabriels first appears as a place name in the seventeenth century, this being the name of the family who held much land in the Edenbridge area. Roodlands does not appear before 1348, these early forms not showing if this is *rod land* 'the agricultural land of the clearing' or speaking of land equal to one rood. Gilridge comes from Old English *glaed hrycg*, recorded as Gladerugg in 1202 this is 'the bright or gleaming ridge of land'. Howlets takes its name from John de Holegh, here by 1304, while a family named Seyliard are recorded at what is now known as Syliards in the twelfth century.

Shernden is from *scearn denn* or 'the woodland pasture where dung is collected'. Stangrove Park is seen as Staingraue in 1270, this from Old English *stan graf* meaning 'the grove of trees at stony ground'. Uphill Farm might seem quite obvious, and yet the records from 1292 as Wyppingwell and from 1357 as Wyppinwelle show this to be derived from Old English *wielle* with a Saxon personal name, giving 'the stream associated with a man called Wippa'. Both Great Browns and Little Browns can be traced to the thirteenth century when a family by the name of Le Brun were in residence. Skeynes is manorial, the name first recorded in the seventeenth century. Crockham Hill stands on a busy road, this thoroughfare being known for 'the homestead where pots were made'.

An attractive sign for Crockham Hill's village hall

Holy Trinity Church at Crockham Hill

Eltham

Domesday records this name as Elteham, here is an Old English place name with two possible meanings. Either this is from *elfitu hamm* and 'the hemmed-in land of the river meadow frequented by swans' or, should the first element be a personal name, 'the homestead of a man called Elta'.

Erith

A name recorded as Earhyth in the middle of the tenth century and as Erhede in Domesday. Here Old English *ear hyth* spoke of this as 'the muddy or gravelly landing place'.

Friday Hill appears as Fridayeshole in 1544. There are two schools of thought when this particular day of the week appears in a place name. When found in relation to a street or way it would point to this being where fish was sold or transported, Friday being the traditional day for serving fish. However here the suffix appears to be Middle English *hole*, in which case it would be a warning of ill-luck for Friday was considered the most unlucky of days in earlier centuries.

Northumberland Heath takes its name from a small stream south of here formerly known as the North Humber, first documented as such in 1292. This was once a fairly common river name, from a Celtic word related to Old Welsh *hu* or 'good' and a word akin to Latin *imber* meaning 'shower'. This water course has topographical evidence which supports the idea from the name to show this was once much broader.

While a link between the local pub and the church may seem odd today, in times when almost everyone worked the land these were the only two places where one would meet other residents of the parish on a regular basis. Furthermore many pubs would find themselves sited on land held by the church. In Erith is one of a number of pubs in England called the Cross Keys, this being the symbol associated with St Peter, although what links him to the pub is not clear.

The Lord Raglan is named after the man who fought in the Peninsula Wars and was military secretary to the Duke of Wellington. He was also commander-in-chief of the British forces in the Crimea, although his officers and men were not exactly generous with their compliments during this campaign. In the Running Horse we see a reference to the wild horses which once roamed the marshland here. Advertising the playing of the traditional pub game of skittles, the Corner Pin is named after the skittle which is the most difficult to knock over while also pointing to the location of the premises.

A sizable dockyard stood at what is now Riverside Gardens in the fifteenth and sixteenth centuries. Indeed one of the most famous warships of the Tudor age, *Henri Grace a Dieu* was fitted out here in 1515. Whilst we have little information on the size of the dock, we do know the size of this vessel. Also known as the Great Harry, she was four decks high, had an overall length of 165 feet, had a minimum weight of 1,000 tons and a complement anywhere between 700 and 1,000.

Eynsford

Listed as Aeinesford around the middle of the tenth century, this name comes from a Saxon or Jute personal name and Old English *ford* and refers to 'the ford of a man called Aegen'.

Eynsford fingerpost

Upper Austin Lodge and Lower Austin Lodge take their names from their respective positions in 'the valley of a man called Ordric', the earliest surviving record coming from 1195 as Orchesden. Cacketshill Wood is on land owned by the family of Roger Cacote de Eynesford by 1345. Hulberry is first found in a document dated 1348, this is from a Saxon personal name and Old English *burh* and gives 'the stronghold of a man called Hielte'. Sparepenny Lane probably began as a nickname for a field, a reference to a low rent.

A delightful Eysnford road name

Early records of Maplescombe show this is not from *mapuldores combe* 'the valley of the maple trees' but from *mapuldores camp* 'the field marked or bordered by maple trees'. Pedham Court is derived from *pytt ham* and describes 'the homestead by a pit', the name recorded from the early thirteenth century. Polly Shaw can be traced back to the thirteenth century, this from *pol haeg* and referring to 'the hedged enclosure near a pool'. Pub names include the Malt Shovel, a large wooden implement used in the brewing process, and the Plough, an invitation to those who worked the land.

The Plough at Eysnford

Eynsford Castle was home to William de Eynsford in the late twelfth century. The two most powerful men in the country at the time were, not surprisingly, Archbishop of Canterbury Thomas Becket and and the English king Henry

II. When Thomas excommunicated William de Eynsford, it was seemingly inevitable the king would use his power to overrule this decision. This row escalated and led to the eventual murder of the man of the church in 1170.

Eysnford's bridge and ford in the foreground

Eythorne

A name derived from a Saxon or Jute personal name and Old English *thorn*. Here is 'the ford of a man called Aegen', the name recorded as Heagythethorne in the ninth century.

Ashley to the east is found from the thirteenth century, the name meaning 'the woodland clearing by or among the ash trees'. Brimsdale Farm, found as Brynessole in 944 and as Bremesdal in 1254, describes this region as 'the muddy pool of a man called Bryni'. From a Saxon or Jute personal name and Old English *tun* comes Elvington or 'the farmstead of a woman called Aelfgythe' and recorded since the eleventh century.

Malmains can be traced back to one family, that headed by Henry Malemeins who were here in 1261. Studdal comes from Old English *stud weald* to tell of 'the cleared woodland where a stud farm is situated'. There are no early records of Waddling Hill Plantation, for this is a transferred name. Just a few short miles away once stood the settlement of Wadling. Now lost its original meaning was 'the place of the family or followers of a man called Waedel'. Waldershare is found in Domesday as Walwalesere, this from *weald wara scearu* or 'the boundary place of the dwellers in the now cleared forest'.

Off Coldred Road is woodland known locally as Thommies Wood. This is a very recent name resulting from this being used by British soldiers training here during the First World War and evidence of the trenches can still be made out in places. This comes from the nickname used for all British soldiers, Tommy Atkins, itself thought to have been derived from the name shown on a specimen form issued by the War Office in 1815.

CHAPTER SIX – F

Farleigh (East & West)

Two places which have a common origin, the additions need no explanation. Here Old English *fearn leah* combine to speak of 'the woodland clearing overgrown with ferns'. The earliest record dates from the ninth century as Fearnlege.

East Farleigh sign

Locally we find Kettle Corner, almost equidistant between the two Farleighs, and a place on a narrow road belonging to a family called Ketyl from around 1374. Doubtless Pimp's Court has produced more than a smirk over the years and yet the origin is akin to the modern 'pimple' for it is used to mean 'swelling'. Doubtless this is the rounded hill on which it stands. Tutsham Hall is seen as Tutesham in 1279 and Tutsham in 1610, where a Saxon personal name with *ham* speaks of 'the homestead of a man called Tutt'.

The pub named the Tickled Trout is a reminder of an old method of catching this food fish. It is exactly what it says, the belly of the trout is tickled and it moves backwards and is caught with the fingers in the gills. It was a method used by poachers as it requires no equipment, thus a lack of evidence should gamekeepers or officers of the law stumble upon them. For this reason it is illegal in Britain.

Barges needing to negotiate Rochester Bridge adopted a most ingenious approach so as not to lose too much headway. Calling in at Whitewall Creek they would collect extra crewmen known as Hufflers who would help build up speed until, at the very last moment, would help to lower the mast using the winch. As soon as the barge emerged on the opposite side they would help to raise the mast once more and be dropped off at either Janes Creek or Temple Creek to await their next barge.

East Farleigh Signpost

Farnborough

A name meaning 'the hill or mound growing with ferns', it is derived from Old English *fearn beorg* and is listed as Ferenberga in 1180.

Many pub names advertise themselves as a rest stop in the days of the coaching routes, although in the case of the Change of Horses the name is likely unique.

Farningham

Listed as Ferningeham in the Domesday record of 1086, this name comes from Old English *fearn inga ham* and describes 'the homestead of the dwellers among the ferns'.

Calfstock is seen as Kalewanstocce in 944 and Calovestok in 1344, this from Old English *aet paem calewan stocce* and a very specific description of this as being 'at the bare stock or tree stump'. Charton is recorded as the modern form as early as 1464, this from the family listed as both Ceriton and Cheriton, landholders by the thirteenth century. Vineyard Shaw is listed as Nethere Vynhagh in 1357, the basic name from *fin haeg* 'the enclosure at the heap'.

Fawkham Green

Listed as Fealcnaham in the tenth century and as Fuchesham in the Domesday record of 1086. Originally this name comes from Old English *ham* and a Saxon or Jute personal name, thus telling of 'the homestead of a man called Fealcna'. The addition comes much later, is from Middle English and refers to the village green.

Fordcombe

Recorded as Ffyrecoumbe in 1313, the origin of this name is in Old English *fyre cumb* or 'the valley of the fir trees'. The obvious name change, which does seem deliberate, would be due to its close proximity to the Medway.

Locally we find Chafford Park, the name from Old English *ceap ford* or 'the ford near where a market is held', the name also seen in the Chafford Arms.

Frindsbury

Recorded as Freonesberiam in 764 and as Frandesberie in the Domesday survey of 1986, this name is derived from a Saxon or Jute personal name and Old English *burh* which speak of 'the stronghold of a man called Freond'.

Bill Street is literally 'the sword-like road', a reference to the straight Roman road recorded as Bilstrete in 1372 and Byll Streete in 1572.

CHAPTER SEVEN – G

Gillingham

Records of this name include Gyllingeham in the tenth century and as Gelingeham in the Domesday survey. Here is a Saxon or Jute personal name and Old English *inga ham*, together telling of 'the homestead of the family or followers of a man called Gylla'.

Street names begin with Britton Street, named after the Brutin family who were here by 1254. Brompton, always pronounced Brumton, comes from Old English *brom tun* or 'the farmstead where broom trees grow'. Capston is seen as Kebbeliston in 1254, this describing 'the *tun* or farmstead of a man called Cybbel'. Darland is a name found as Dirilaunde in 1254 and as Derlond in 1450, this being from Old English *deor land* 'the agricultural land frequented by wild animals'. Gadshill is the name of a Christian place of worship, Old English *godes hyll* speaking of this place as 'God's hill'. Whetstead appears in a ninth century document as Hwaetanstede and comes from *hwaeten stede* or 'the place where wheat grows'.

Great Lines began as the name of a hill, an eighteenth century earthwork constructed as part of the defences during the Napoleonic Wars. Woodlands is seen as Wodelonde in 1327, this from *wudu land* and speaking of 'the agricultural land near a wood'. Twydall comes from Old English *twidael* meaning 'double portion' or perhaps 'double dole', either way it meant the tenant had to pay twice as much for having twice the normal area of land.

Pub names include the Golden Lion, another of the oddly coloured animals which show this is heraldic. Such a powerful image has been chosen by many powerful families, including Henry I and, most often, the Percy family, dukes of Northumberland. The Hop and Vine advertises the product, the former used to brew beer, the latter giving wines. The Two Sawyers became a pub name despite it not being heraldic, the sawyer was not considered a skilled profession and therefore not granted arms.

In the Canterbury Tales we find a name referring to the title of the book where a collection of stories tells of the pilgrims journeying to Canterbury to visit the tomb of St Thomas a Becket. A general invitation is offered by the Dewdrop Inn. The Viscount Hardinge is named after the Kent-born man who served in the army under the Duke of Wellington, later following him as commander-in-chief of the British Army and later in a political career which saw him serve in parliament and as governor general in India. Another military career gave a name to the Royal Marine, while a general reference gave a name to the Army and Navy public house.

The Burnt Oak is a name found in many places across the country. While burning the tree will kill it, as the massive heartwood of the oak will remain untouched the blackened remains will stand for years as a signpost. The Green Dragon is heraldic, the name always pointing to the earls of Pembroke, once major landholders. Naming the King George V will have been due to it being opened sometime during the reign which lasted from 1910 to early 1936.

A unique name was created when a local brewery decided to amalgamate two pubs, the Lord Nelson and the Steam Engine. Many suggestions were put forward and eventually the Spyglass and Kettle was chosen, the former used by the greatest naval hero of them all, the latter once a colloquial name for a steam locomotive.

Goddington

Documented as Godinton in 1240, this represents a Saxon personal name and Old English *ing tun* telling of 'the farmstead associated with a man called Goda'.

Goudhurst

Found as Guithyrste in the eleventh century, here is a name from a Saxon or Jute personal name and Old English *hyrst* which informs us this was 'the wooded hill of a man called Gutha'.

Ballards is a name associated with the family of Richard Ballard, who were certainly here by 1642. Combourne comes from *cumb burna* 'the stream in the valley', probably fed by Combwell 'the valley spring'. Etchinghill is a corruption of Tottingehol in 1254, Totingehole in 1270, and Totinghole mill in 1333, the name also seen in nearby Etchinghole. Unfortunately later records are unavailable, thus the evolution to the present form is a mystery. However there can be no doubt the two are the same, this meaning 'the *hol* or hollow of the people of a man called Totta'. Taywell comes from Old English *taeg wielle* and tells of 'the spring at the enclosure'.

Hammond's Farm was connected with the Hammon family for the first time in 1642 when Mary Hammon was documented as being head of the household. Paine's Farm can be traced to 1348 when it was associated with a family called Payn. Records of Pickenden are a little late, making it difficult to tell if this is 'the woodland pasture of a man called Pinca' or, should the first element not be a personal name, 'the woodland pasture frequented by finches'. Worms Hill is listed as Wormeshelle in 1327, this certainly represents *wyrm hyll* but could either speak of 'the hill frequented by snakes' or Wyrm might be used as a personal name. Chingley, found as Chingele around the end of the twelfth century and as Chingeleghe in 1253, is derived from Middle English *cingel legh* and describes 'the woodland clearing where shingles are obtained'.

Riseden is from *hris denn* and seen as Rysdenne in the early thirteenth century. This Old English name speaks of this place as 'the woodland pasture marked by brushwood'. Ruckhurst Wood is possibly named after the lord of the manor in the reign of Henry I. One William Rookherst, said to be from Scotland, built the mansion house here at that time. Less likely, but equally plausible, the man took his name from an existing and previously unrecorded place name. The latter would come from Old English *hroc hyrst* or 'the wooded hill frequented by rooks'. Brandfold has a second element from *falod* 'fold', although the first part has proven difficult. An obsolete *brangle* has been suggested meaning 'to totter', in which case this is understood as 'the dilapidated fold'.

Shearnfold Wood takes its name from *scearn feld* and speaks of 'the open land where dung is collected. Found as Smoghele and Smowelegh in the thirteenth century, Smugley is from *smuge leah* and tells of 'the woodland clearing where creepers abound'. Spoonlets Pond comes from the adjacent *spon leah* or 'woodland clearing where wood chips are collected and/or stored'. Such wood shavings had many uses. Winchet Hill is seen as Wyndschete in 1440, from *wind scete* this is literally 'the wind land' and where the open area allows the wind to blow uninterrupted by natural windbreaks.

Grain

Listed as Grean around 1100, this is from Old English *greon* and describes the 'gravelly or coarse sandy ground'. The Isle of Grain, once an actual island, appears as Ile of Greane in a document dated 1610.

Locally we find St James's Farm, named for it being managed by the local church which was, of course, dedicated to St James. Smithfield Shaw is recorded since the sixteenth century, this from *smethe feld scaga* and describing 'the copse near the smooth open land'.

Here we find the Cat and Cracker, a pub named after the oil refinery in the Thames estuary which operates on a system known as catalytic cracking. The Hogarth remembers William Hogarth, a painter who produced satirical works aimed at raising awareness and the need for social reform.

Grange

Documented as Grenic at the end of the eleventh century, this name is derived from Old English *grene wic* and speaks of 'the green trading place'. While the adjective may seem to be describing somewhere eco friendly, in the pre-Norman era it simply described somewhere with plenty of vegetation.

Gravesend

A name found as Gravesham in 1086 and as Grauessend in 1157, this name comes from Old English *graf ende* and describes the '(place at) the end of the grove'.

The local name of Rosherville recalls one Jeremiah Rosher, a man who designed a place of Victorian perambulation and delight here. Derived from Old English *iw feld* and recorded as Yfeld in 1174, the minor name of Ifield speaks of 'the open land where yew trees are seen'.

The Pelham Arms is a pub name featuring the family who were important landowners as the dukes of Newcastle. A friendly society with branches across the land advertises a meeting place in the name of the Buffalo's Head. At the Call Boy the name was suggested by the pub occupying the site of the former Grand Theatre building. At first the sign showed a boy knocking to alert a performer of their imminent arrival on stage, later it was repainted showing a trumpeter in a military uniform. The Canal Tavern and Canal Street both show the location.

Gravesend's charter permitting the town to hold a market dates from 1268. This makes it one of the oldest surviving markets in the country.

Greenhithe

Found as Grenethe in 1264, this name comes from Old English *grene hyth* and tells us it was 'the green landing place'. As stated under the entry for Grange this refers to vegetation.

Knockhall is a local name from Old English *aet thaem ac holte* or 'at the oak thicket', the name first seen as Nockholte in 1332.

The pub name and sign is an advertisement, an invitation to imbibe and perhaps feast within. There is no doubting just who is invited in the name of the Welcome All.

Greenwich

While Old English *wic* is most often defined as 'specialised farm', and that speciality is nearly always dairy produce, this is not always the message being conveyed and here is one example. From *grene wic* and recorded as Grenewic in 964 and as Grenviz in 1086, this describes 'the green port or harbour', telling us the land around here was noticably green.

In the early eleventh century the Danes anchored in the Thames off Greenwich and remained there for three years. They camped on the hill at Greenwich and launched an attack on Canterbury, taking Alphege, Archbishop of Canterbury, prisoner and demanding a ransom. When Alphege refused to allow the payment of three thousand pieces of silver for his release, his captors stoned him to death. However they had a change of heart when a stick, which had been soaking in his blood, suddenly bloomed and the seeming miracle saw his body returned to his followers.

Groombridge

A name derived from a combination of Middle English *grome* and Old English *brycg* and speaks of 'the bridge where young men congregate'. While history does not record why the men were gathering here, it does tell show the place as Gromenebregge in 1239.

CHAPTER EIGHT – H

Hadlow

Listed as Haslow in 1086 and as Hadlou in 1235, this name comes from Old English *haeth hlaw* and describes 'the mound or hill where heather grows'.

Blackman's Lane is derived from the family of Blakeman, first recorded here in the thirteenth century. Falklands is named after Viscountess Falkland, documented as a landowner in a document dated 1768. Great Fish Hall and Little Fish Hall share an origin, a reminder of the family of Ffisher or Fyshher, here by the seventeenth century. In 1348 the Geman family are recorded at what is now known as Gammon's Land.

Ouseley comes from Old English *wase leah* and influenced by Middle English *wos leghe* both of which literally mean 'the ooze clearing' and a reference to a muddy place. North Frith features the element *fyrhthe* 'woodland' and was north' of the now lost place name of South Frith. Parker's Green can be traced to a document from 1292 when it is first associated with the family of William le Parker.

Outside the Artichoke Inn the image of this vegetable shows how easily recognisable it is. However prior to the sixteenth century no artichoke had ever been seen in England, although it soon became known for its distinctive appearance and was often used to advertise produce markets or seed merchants.

Halling

Found as Hallingas in the eighth century and as Hallinges in Domesday, this name comes from a Saxon or Jute personal name and Old English *ingas* and tells us of the '(place of) the family or followers of a man called Heall'.

Bavins Shaw takes its name from the Bavent family, who held Halling in the thirteenth and fourteenth centuries. Cannon Wood is named for the family of John Canoun, here by 1327. Pastead Wood is found as Perstede in 1334, a name from *peru stede* or 'the place where pears grow'.

The Pilgrims Rest is almost a predictable pub name at Upper Halling. Those heading for the shrine of St Thomas a Becket at Canterbury being offered refreshment here. In the Black Boy we probably find a reference to the chimney sweeps featured in many Dickens novels, however it should also be noted the name became popular two hundred years before the author was born. It then referred to the black page boys who, dressed in brightly coloured, often striped, attire were fashionable companions and servants.

Halstead

Documented at the end of the eleventh century as Haltesteda, here is an Old English place name derived from *heald* and telling us it was 'the place of refuge, a shelter'.

Cadlocks is seen as home to the family of John Kedelak in 1327. Colgates is from Old English *col geat* literally 'the charcoal way' and pointing to a route into woodland where charcoal was burned. Fairtrough is first seen in 1254, this from *faeger treow* or 'the beautiful tree'.

Hartley

The second example of this place name in Kent, this being found near Longfield. Recorded as Erclei in 1086 and as Hertle in 1253, this has the same origin as the previous entry, coming from Old English *heorot leah* it again describes 'the woodland clearing frequented by harts or stags'.

The local name of Fairby is derived from the Hartley family of John Feerby, here by 1420. However the influence of the earlier Fairfield cannot be denied, this first seen in the thirteenth century as Faierfeld, Feyrefeld and Fairefeld, Old English *faeger feld* telling of 'the fair open land'.

Hawley

Domesday lists this name as Hagelei in 1086 and is seen again in 1203 as Halgeleg. Here Old English *halig leah* tells us of 'the holy woodland clearing'.

Clement Street takes the name of former residents, the Clement family recorded here in 1327, while there is also a place name Clementeslond seen in 1374.

Hayes

One of two places of this name in the county, this example is found near Bromley. Listed as Hesa in 1177, this comes from Old English *haese* and describes 'the land overgrown with brushwood'.

Baston Farm gets its name from *baecstane* or 'backstone', the flat broad stones which were heated by the fire from beneath and radiated the heat into the oven.

Hayes

The second example of this name is near Hillingdon. Again from Old English *haese* this is 'the land overgrown with brushwood' and is seen as Haese in 831 and as Hesa in 1086.

Hever

Listed as Heanyfre in 814, this comes from Old English *heah yfer* and describes the '(place at) the high edge or brow of a ridge'.

Bramsell's Farm is from *bremel syle* or 'the miry place where brambles abound'. Brocas is a reminder of the Brokey family who were associated with this area by 1347, their name later seen as Brokas in 1383. How Green appears as Hokegrene in 1440, this referring to the *hoc* or 'hook of land'. Polebrook stands alongside the river and certainly merits a name meaning 'marshy ground at the pools'. From *pol broc* this is recorded as Polebroc in 1240 and as Polbroke in 1347. Uckfield Wood was ultimately named from its namesake in Sussex, however it was brought here as a surname with one John le Bakere de Vkkefelde here at the end of the thirteenth century.

When it comes to pub names, one would think one of the last names to be chosen for a pub in Hever would be the King Henry VIII. While he did make her his second wife he also trumped up charges of incest and treason in order to have her beheaded, and Anne Boleyn had grown up here.

Higham

A name meaning the 'high or chief homestead'. This name comes from Old English *heah ham* and is first recorded as Hegham in 1242.

Both Abbey Farm and Abbey Wood recall Higham Priory, a Benedictine priory established in 1148. Barrowhill has two elements referring to the same feature, the 'barrow hill'. Merston has not changed since the record from 1242, however these records date back to 774 when the name appears as *mersc tun* 'the farmstead of or by the marsh'.

A ballad entitled *The Robbers of Gad's Hill* was certainly known by 1558. This told of the infamous haunt in Higham at Gad's Hill and achieved such notoriety it was used by the Bard of Avon himself. In Shakespeare's *Henry IV Part 1*, Falstaff and his men rob travellers here but do not get away with their ill-gotten gains, Prince Hal relieving them of their spoils.

Higham Upshire

Found as Heahhaam around 765 and as Hecham in 1086, this name comes from Old English *heah ham* and 'the chief or high homestead'. The addition, to distinguish it from the other Highams, is from *upp scir* and refers to 'the higher district'.

Gadshill is derived from Old English *godes hyll*, the record of 973 as Godes hylle being little different, describing the Christian place of worship as 'God's hill'. Taylor's Lane can be traced to the early fourteenth century when John and Thomas Taillour were resident here.

High Brooms

Records of this name include as Bromgeburg in 1270 and as Bromelaregg in 1318. Undoubtedly the first element here is Old English *brom*, however it is difficult to tell from these late forms if this is *brom brycg* and 'the bridge where broom grows', or if this represents *brom hrycg* and 'the ridge where broom grows'.

Hildenborough

Listed as Hyldenn in 1240 and as Hildenborough as early as 1389, these records show the name changed slightly in the invervening one hundred and fifty years. Originally from Old English *hyll dean* and describing 'the woodland pasture on or by a hill', the later form adds *burh*, used here to mean manor, borough'.

Philpott's Cross is named after the family of Thomas Philpott, first documented here in the early sixteenth century. Bassett's Mill takes the name of the family of John Bassett, who were recorded here in 1377. One local name is Nizel, also seen as Nizel's Heath, which comes from *nige gesella* or 'the new buildings' which we must assume were very evident. Watt's Cross Road is derived from the family of John Watte, who were living at the crossroads here by 1327.

Outside the local of the Flying Dutchman we see a sign depicting the origin in the fabled ghostly ship said to be seen off the Cape of Good Hope. Doomed to sail the ocean forever and never reach port, seeing it is held to be a bad omen.

Hoo St Werburgh

As with the previous listing the basic name comes from Old English *hoh* meaning the '(place at) the spur of land'. The addition, once again, refers to the dedication of the church.

Locally we find Abbot's Court, once the property of the Abbey of Boxley. Broad Street is self-explanatory, a name recorded since the early fourteenth century when it would have seemed much broader than it does today. Huggin's Wood derives its name from the family of John Huggin, here by 1634.

Horsmonden

Listed as Horsbundenne around the end of the eleventh century, this name comes from Old English *hors burna denn* and tells us it was 'the woodland pasture near the stream where horses drank'.

Bainden is found as Beginden in 1254, this being 'the *denn* or woodland pasture of a man called Baega'. From Old English *becge broc* comes Baybrooks, a name meaning 'the marsh in a bend'. Brambles Farm and Brambles Place, both originating in 'the place where brambles grow', here take the name of the family of William Brembil, here by 1324. The Chart takes its name from *cert* meaning 'rough common'.

Horsmonden village sign

Gafford's Bridge is recorded as Gatesford in 1313 and Garteforde in 1344, from Old English *gates ford* the 'ford across which goats are herded' would have been across a tributary of the Beult. Grovehurst is documented as Grofhurste in 1240, Old English *graf hyrst* describing 'the grove of the wooded hill'. Hayman's Hill was Hammons Hill in 1782, likely a reminder of the family of Haymond, here by the fourteenth century. Ram's Hill is a lasting reminder of the family named Ram recorded here in the latter half of the fourteenth century.

Hazel Street appears as Haesl holte in 964 and as Aisiholte in 1086, this from *haesel* and, as the name still says today, 'where hazel trees grow'. Lewis Heath is a Saxon name although 'the heathland of a man called Leof' is not recorded as a place name before 1240. Smallbridge is self-explanatory, the name having been in use since at least the sixteenth century. Spelmonden Road comes from Old English *spilemanning denn* and literally meaning 'the woodland pasture of the player'. While we can never know exactly what was played, we do know it was not games or sports for a *spilemann* was a jester or musician.

Sprivers is found from the sixteenth century, yet the name dates from at least 1310 when this is first seen as a surname with the arrival of John Speruer and later Robert Spriver in 1447. Stammerden Wood is from Old English *stan manning denn*, recorded since the thirteenth century and telling of 'the

woodland pasture of the stone masons'. Stunts Wood can be traced to 1235 when the family of Sidney Stunt were first recorded here. Broad Ford speaks for itself, although the early records also show the name as Brodeford mylle, pointing out there was once a watermill here.

Horsmonden fingerpost

Horton Kirby

Domesday lists this name as Hortune in 1086, later seen as Horton Kyekeby in 1346. The basic name comes from Old English *horu tun* and speaks of 'the dirty or muddy farmstead'. Here the addition is manorial, showing possession by the de Kirkeby family by the thirteenth century. Franks is named after the family who held this land, also during the thirteenth century.

Pub names include the Fighting Cocks, a name showing these premises were a regular venue for the so-called sport of cock fighting. Introduced by the Romans, large sums of money were wagered on the outcome. When steps were taken to banish this cruel sport it went underground until the mid-nineteenth century when sterner measures were taken to eradicate it completely. In the Bull is a pub name, one which has two sources used equally and very difficult to split. Hence this is either a name derived from a favourite or champion beast, or the animal was chosen to represent a family heraldically.

Hunton

Found as Huntindone in the eleventh century, this is derived from Old English *hunta dun* and refers to this as 'the hill of the huntsmen'.

Amsbury Wood is first seen in 1264 as Ambresbir, this being 'the stronghold of a man called Aembre'. Buston is recorded as Burricestune and Burgericestune in the twelfth century, this being 'the *tun* or farmstead of a man called Burgric'. Fisher's Wood recalls the family of John Ffysshere, who were certainly here by 1352.

Hunton's village sign

Hunton fingerpost

CHAPTER NINE – I

Ide Hill

Found in a document from around the middle of the thirteenth century as Edythehelle, this name comes from a Saxon or Jute personal name and Old English *hyll* and speaks of 'the hill of a woman called Edith'. A name of similar manorial origins is found nearby, but with Toys Hill no records have survived to show the family name involved.

Boarhill is certainly a transferred name, however whether this came from the estate of Bore Place of the family name Bore, they held this place from 1313, is uncertain. Bore Place itself comes from *bur* or 'bower'. Everlands is found as Everlaund in 1239, this coming from *eofor land* or ''the agricultural land frequented by wild boar'. Whitley Forest is recorded as Whitehell in 1313, this referring to it being 'at the white hill', with the temporary change of this chalk land to 'the white cliff' from a record of Whytclyffe in 1535. Henden is from *haen denn* and, recorded as Handenne in the early fourteenth century, describes 'the high woodland pasture'.

Ightham

Listed at the end of the eleventh century as Ehteham, this name comes from a Saxon or Jute personal name and Old English *ham* and speaks of 'the homestead of a man called Ehta'. In the nearby name of Haytham Green we see the same origin but one which has evolved quite differently.

Bewley Farm is of Old French origin, found as Beauley in 1521 and Beaulies in 1782 this represents *beau lieu* or 'the beautiful place'. Ivy Hatch is from Old English *hefig haecc* and speaks of 'the heavy hatch gate'. If we rely on records of Patchgrove Wood alone it would seem to be a recent name dating from around the eighteenth century. However the origin of the name, telling of 'the irregularly shaped grove in a wood', suggests it is much older. Scathes Wood is first seen in the fourteenth century, the name describing 'the dwellers at the boundary'.

The Chequers Inn is one of the oldest known pub names, with evidence of this being unearthed in the streets of Pompeii following the eruption in ad79. Originally used to show a board game was played within, it was later used to indicate a the landlord also acted as a moneyer. Today that image and name continues to represent fiscal matters in the form of the title with the person with his hands on the financial reins of the country, the Chancellor of the Exchequer. The sign outside the Cob Tree shows a cob horse standing by a cob-nut tree, the latter the true origin of the pub name.

Isle of Dogs

This place name is not known before the 1593 record of Isle of Dogs Ferm. Here the message is probably as simple as it seems and describes 'the peninsula in a marsh frequented by wild (or feral) dogs'.

Not that this ever stops speculation as to the origin of the name, indeed there are almost a dozen suggestions as to the beginning of the name. For example this was where Edward III kept and/or exercised his greyhounds, although this breed was more commonly known as a gazehound at this time, so-called because they honed in on their prey by sight rather than smell. Some sources say this is a corruption of the Isle of Ducks, again unlikely as ducks were found everywhere.

John Strype says it was a nickname, one which tells us it was a dog's life for anyone who lived here, perhaps supported by Samuel Pepys who described this place as 'the unlucky Isle of Dogs'. Another idea is this referred to Dutch engineers who helped reclaim the land from the sea following record high tides and the resulting floods. Similarly this is a corruption of 'Isle of Dykes'. There is also the thought it might refer to the gibbets and their occupants, who would have been the 'dogs'. No records have been discovered to back the idea of a yeoman farmer by the name of Brache once worked this land, this being a nickname and a term describing a breed of hunting dog. One of the more ludicrous ideas is this was derived from the number of dead dogs washed up on the banks of the river Thames. Almost as creative is the notion this referred to the metal fire dogs unloaded at the docks. Perhaps this was a reminder of the hunting dogs of Henry VIII, who was known to hunt deer in the nearby park.

CHAPTER TEN – K

Kemsing

Found as Cymesing in 822, this name comes from a Saxon or Jute personal name and Old English *ing* and describes 'the place of a man called Cymesa'.

Kemsing fingerpost

Greenland Shaw does mean 'the grass-covered agricultural land' with the addition of *scaga* or 'copse', at least as a part of the place name, not seen until the eighteenth century. Haversham is a hamlet derived from *eofor hamm*, a name describing 'the water meadow frequented by wild boar'. St Clere may seem to have religious connections and yet nothing could be further from the truth. A document dated 1346 gives the answer, for this shows a family headed by one Isolda Seyntclere in residence. Exactly the opposite is the case with St Edith's Farm. This was named from St Edith's Well, itself suggested by the belief that this woman was born in the village, although there is little evidence to support this. Eatwell Shaw is a *scaga* or 'copse' added to a basic name which is a corruption of St Edith's Well found in the centre of Kemsing.

At the Wheatsheaf the sign displays the image suggested by the name. This is taken from a coat of arms, most obviously that of the Brewers Company but is also representative of the Worshipful Company of Bakers. Both are equally plausible as early landlords could never have made a living from brewing alone, thus often took on the role of a second tradesman, such as a baker.

In 961 Kemsing was the birthplace of St Edith of Wilton, although at the time she was just another illegitimate child of the Saxon king, Edgar I. There is a well at the centre of the village which bears her name and a plaque telling how she was responsible for the healing properties of its waters. Her statue adorns the front of St Edith's Hall, together with a clock which chimes the hours for the residents of Kemsing.

Kemsing street name

Kennington

Listed in Domesday as Chenetone, this record tells us the name comes from Old English *cyne tun* and describes 'the king's or royal farmstead'.

Great Burton and Little Burton have a common origin in *byre tun* or 'the farmstead with a cattle byre', not the normal definition for this common English place name. East Mountain Farm comes from *east manna tun*, telling of 'the farmstead of the east men'. Kempe's Corner comes from the family of John Kempe, recorded here in 1334.

Kent

The name of the county is first seen in 51bc as Cantium. Clearly this is an ancient Celtic name, although the actual meaning is uncertain but has been explained most often as 'the coastal district' or alternatively 'land of the armies'.

Keston

Seen as Cysse stan in 973 and as Chestan in 1086, here is a Saxon personal name and Old English *stan* and referring to 'the boundary stone of a man called Cyssi'.

The local name of Crittenden is recorded as Westguterindenne in 1227, Guteringden in 1258 and as Crotynden in 1451. This name describes itself as 'the woodland pasture of a man called Guthhere', although why it should have attracted the additional 'west' in the thirteenth century record is a mystery.

Among the most common pub names in the land, the Fox is as often seen coupled with a second item or creature and is also seen on its own. The animal is also a common sight, its distinctive coat and features making for an attractive sign. It is almost always impossible to say why the image was chosen with any certainty. When it comes to the Greyhound the image is from the coat of arms of the dukes of Newcastle, major landowners in the country.

Kidbrooke

The earliest known record of this name dates from 1202 as Ketebroc. This name is derived from Old English *cyta broc* and speaks of 'the brook where kites are seen'. The Kyd Brook is a tributary of the Ravensbourne, running between Orpington and Lewisham. Yet by the time it reaches the latter it is known as the River Quaggy, an interesting point when it comes to the development of river names.

Here the brook is named after the bird of prey, and while this bird of prey would have had a large range it would not be confined to the course of the river, after all it is not a water bird. It is quite safe to assume the bird was seen as often around the river Quaggy as at Kidbrooke, the former name describing the area as 'muddy', and to find different names for the same water course is to be expected. In earlier times travel was time-consuming and took manpower away from the fields and avoided by most except when trading.

Just as place names described a specific point, so did river names. What was a fast running young river in the Cotswolds, grows to become a large tidal estuary on the east coast, this England's longest river and the Thames has many other faces during the 220 miles from source to sea. Undoubtedly this river had many names at various points over the centuries, while today there is but one, known as the Isis as it flows through Oxford.

Almost every name became fixed when it was written about. In the case of river names this would have been in the form of a map, and as rivers formed fixed points of reference it made sense to draw these in first. In the case of major rivers such as the Thames, the name appears on maps of the country and quickly becomes accepted as the 'real' name – it is quite astonishing to find the Thames still known as the Isis at Oxford – while the cartographer at Kidbrook and another at Lewisham were working on a much smaller region and including landmarks which the larger scale could never show.

In Kidbrook and Lewisham both cartographers ask the locals the name of the river before marking such on their respective maps. Normally one name will continue while others eventually fall out of use and disappear off the map. In the case of the Kyd/Quaggy the brook/river is small enough to have retained both names, not unique but quite rare.

Knockholt

Records of this name include as Ocholt in 1197 and as Nocjolt in 1353. This is from Old English *a holt* which describes this as the '(place at) the oak tree wood'. That this name has come to begin with first N and now K is initially due to the Old English definite article and later through the accepted spelling of Knock- rather than Nock-.

Cudham is recorded as Codeham in Domesday and as Codham in 1269, this being 'the *ham* or homestead of a man called Cuda'. A lost manor known as Bertrey, from *beorht ea* or 'the bright stream', was transferred to neighbouring Berry's Green. Aperfield Court is from *apulder feld* 'the open land of or near the apple trees'. From Old English *scid denn* comes Skid Hill, telling us it was 'the woodland pasture where slips of wood were collected (as fuel)'.

Biggin Hill is a famous name synonymous with flight, yet the name dates from a time when air travel was for the birds and the gods. This represents Middle English *bigging strete* 'the Roman road passing a building', this being the road to (or from) Dover. From Old English *loca stede*, Lusted speaks of itself as 'the enclosed place'. Lett's Green can be traced to a document dated 1332, when it was associated with the family of Galfridus Lete.

The Nower has come from Middle English *atten ore* to describe this as being 'at the bank of land'. Shelleys Lane can be traced to the fourteenth century, when a family were recorded here and in particular two individuals, Thomas de Schelvelegh and Thomas Shelleghe, with rather different spellings for the surname. Stoneings Lane can be traced back to at least 1254 when the family of Robert de Stanhengh was recorded as living here.

The Tally Ho public house shows a connection to the hunt, this being the cry sent up when the quarry was sighted. As to the origins of the phrase 'tally ho' there are numerous suggestions, all of which are doubtful at best.

CHAPTER ELEVEN – L

Lamberhurst

Recorded as Lamburherste in a document dating from the end of the eleventh century, this name comes from Old English *lamb hyrst* and describes 'the wooded hill where lambs are grazed'.

Lamberhurst village sign

Bayham is first recorded in 1228 as Begeham, this being 'the hemmed-in land of a man called Baega'. Bewlbridge, which did indeed cross the River Bewl, was corrupted by the river name and has a different origin. Records include Beldebrigg in 1313, Beauldbridge in 1576, and Beaulbridge in 1596, which show the evolution form what began as 'the bridge of a man called Bealde'.

Crowhurst unites two Old English elements, *crawe scyrte* describes 'the shortened area of land frequented by crows'. This has become corrupted to Crowhurst and probably for no other reason than this is the more common name. Finchcocks is a house first seen in a document dated 1782, named from the family of Finchecock who owned this manor from the middle of thirteenth century. Hayden Wood is seen as Heah daen in 838, little different from the original Old English *heah denn*, showing how it is important to find as early a record as possible, telling of the 'high woodland pasture'.

Kilndown comes from Old English *cylene dun* 'the kiln on a hill'. This must have been named from the view it gave on the skyline to others, for kilns were built on top of a slope as it provided a natural updraft which fuelled the fire. Lindridge comes from Old English *lind hrycg* and describes 'the ridge where lime trees grow'. Scotney Castle was named after the sixteenth century lords of the manor, the barons de Scotini who took their name from Scotigny in France.

Langley

A name which is common to many counties, always coming from Old English *lang leah* and referring to the 'long woodland clearing'. This name is found in a document dating from 814 as Loganleag and as Lanvelei in the Domesday survey.

Brishing Wood and Brishing Court share a name from a personal name and Old English *ingas* or 'the settlement of the family or followers of a man called Broesa', the name listed as Bressinges in 1242 and as Brasinges in 1253. Chartway Street takes its name from *cert weg* 'the way over rough common'. Lested Cottage and Lested Lane gets its name from *leah stede* 'the place of the woodland clearing'.

An easy name to define is that of Bleak House. Instantly a reminder of the novel by Charles Dickens it is clear the two are related when we discover that not only was the novelist resident here but also penned a great proportion of that work here.

Langton Green

A small village to the west of Royal Tunbridge Wells which has no surviving early records whatsoever. Yet it seems highly improbable this is anything but Old English *lang tun* 'the long farmstead'. This is a common enough place name and one which shows the settlement was aligned along the main, and possibly only, road through the village. Had it been aligned along a small side road it would be known as 'the broad farmstead'.

Courtenwell is listed as Corthone in 1327, all the early forms showing this was from Middle English *curt tone* 'the short farmstead' and telling us the settlement was not strung out along a road but clustered closely together. Not until comparatively recently did we see the addition of 'well', nor does there seem any reason for it, particularly not in an etymological sense, hence the water source has no influence on the origins of the place name. Farnham comes from Old English *fearn inga ham* and tells of 'the homestead of the dwellers at the ferns'.

Future developers might like to learn the table-top football game *Subbuteo*, once found in just about every boy's room, was created and made here for many years. Whilst the modern computer game has made such games obsolete, recognition in the form of a street name or two would surely be merited.

Larkfield

A place found in the Domesday record as Lavrochesfel in 1086, this name comes from Old English *lawerce feld* and describes 'the open land frequented by larks'.

To the north of here is New Hythe, a name from Old English *niwe hyth* a name best defined as 'the newer landing place' for it is hardly 'new' being first recorded in 1254. Bellingham is recorded from the tenth century, a Saxon name describing 'the hemmed-in land of the family or followers of a man called Beora'.

Trades are a common choice for a pub name, although why some were chosen is often a mystery. Perhaps a landlord at the Bricklayers Arms had had connections to this trade. In the Monks Head the name refers to George Monk, Duke of Albermarle who is best remembered for his efforts in the Restoration of the Monarchy for which Charles II awarded him the peerage.

Leeds

Domesday records this name as Esledes with an undated but clearly contemporary listing as Hledes, showing this as most likely an old stream name derived from Old English *hlyde* and meaning 'the loud one'.

Brogden is 'the marshy pasture', Old English *broc denn* listed as Brocden by 1285 and as Brokedenn in 1367. Caring is seen as Karynge in 1270 and as Caringe in 1334, this being the '(place of) the family or followers of a man called Caru'. Spout House was built, as the name tells us, at a location where a 'waterspout or conduit' could be found, the name from Middle English *spoute*.

The most famous feature here is undoubtedly Leeds Castle. Standing on an island in a lake created by damming the river Len, what we see today is largely a nineteenth century rebuild. However there has been a castle on this site since 1119, with numerous changes and improvements since then. Former owner Edward I, who considered it one of his favourite places, spent a good deal of money improving this building, while during the sixteenth century Henry VIII gave this to his first wife, Catherine of Aragon.

Since 1952 the building has had Grade I Listing. Since then it has grown to become one of the major tourist attractions in the land. Improvements continue to be made. A maze was constructed, its hedges contain some 2,400 yew trees, for the golfers a course has been laid out, there is also a grotto and, thought to be the only one of its kind in the world, a museum of dog collars.

Leigh

A name which means the '(place at) the woodland clearing' and derived from Old English *leah,* most often seen as a suffix. The name is recorded as Lega in a document from around the end of the eleventh century.

Both Ashour Farm and Ashour Wood share an Old English origin of *aesc ora* 'the bank marked by an ash tree'. Blackhoath Wood is recorded as Blackhethe in 1408 and as Blakhoth in 1438, the earlier form showing this is an unusual corruption of *blaec haeth* 'the dark heathland'. Charcott is seen as Cherecot in 1275 and Cherecote in 1301, from Old English *ceorla cot* this is 'the cottage of the churls or peasants'. Ensfield appears as Jenesfelde in the late twelfth century, it describing 'the *feld* or open land of a man called Geon'.

Cinder Hill comes from *sinder hyll,* Old English for 'the hill where cinders are dumped' and evidence of early iron smelting. Coppings Farm is taken from the family of John Coppyng, here by 1327. In the fourteenth century a family named Kedelak lived here, the name remembered by Killick's Bank. Pauls Farm is found as Polle in 1254, from Middle English *polle* this is named from the 'head or hillock' here. Pubs here include the Bat and Ball, a name showing the long association between Kent and our national summer sport of cricket.

Leigh was also home to the Penshurst Airfield, constructed as a military base but which also worked together with flights in and out of nearby Croydon. On 2 October 1926, a passenger flight got into trouble when a fire broke out on a Bleriot 155. The pilot attempted to make an emergency landing at Penshurst, but sadly the both crew members and five passengers all died in the crash. Only two of these aircraft were ever built, the other crashed in August of the same year. It is recorded as the first accident of its kind aboard an airliner – although this 'airliner' only carried seven people.

Len (River)

The River Len here is named from Lenham, a name meaning 'the homestead of a man called Leana', a process known as back formation. As noted under the entry for the River Eden, this river name must have been known as something else prior to the arrival of the Saxons, although no record survives.

Another point to take into consideration applies to all rivers. Many river names describe the nature of the river or the surrounding countryside. Clearly, and this is true of so many rivers, neither the strength of the river nor the landscape is the same for much of its length. Thus the likelihood is this river had many names, depending on where along its course those who named it were found. Furthermore the modern name would depend on where early cartographers did their research.

Lewisham

Domesday records this name as Levesham in 1086. Here is a Saxon personal name and Old English *ham* speaking of 'the homestead of a man called Leofsa'. Once recorded as La Fforest de Leuesham in 1292, the name of Forest Hill needs no explanation.

The town has migrated since it was founded, for originally it was centred on St Mary's Church. With the coming of the railway, the station being located north of the town, slowly the core of the settlement moved further north. This was not planned but simply a natural occurrence, unlike the building of what was the largest supermarket in Europe when it opened in 1977 but is not big enough to qualify as even average by modern standards. With the building of the police station twenty-five years later, Lewisham could again boast a purpose-built building as the largest of its kind in Europe.

Leybourne

A name derived from a Saxon or Jute personal name and Old English *burna* and telling of 'the stream of a man called Lylla'. Records of this name include as Lillanburna in the tenth century and as Leleburne in Domesday in 1086.

Linton

A place name derived from a Saxon or Jute personal name and Old English *ing tun*, this name speaks of 'the farmstead associated with a man called Lill or Lilla'. The name has lost a syllable over the centuries, being recorded as Lilintuna at the end of the eleventh century.

Loddington Farm is a local name recorded since the fourteenth century, a name referring to 'the *denn* or woodland pasture of a man called Ludel'. Reason Hill remembers 1327, by which time the family of John Reisoun were resident here.

Longfield

With the tenth century listing of Langfelda and in Domesday as Langafel, these show the origin to be Old English *lang feld* which speaks of the 'long stretch of open land'.

Chalkcroft does indeed refer to 'the small holding on chalky soil', recorded as Chalccroft in 1217 and coming from *cealc croft*. Middleton Farm was named after the family associated with it in 1387, these being headed by Richard Middleton. Nurstead is derived from *hnutu stede* and describes 'the place where nuts are found', the name appearing in the Domesday record of 1086. Pinden is found as Pinindene in a document dating from the late tenth century, named from the *dene* or 'valley of a man called Pinna'.

At the Green Man the obvious thought is of the attire of Robin Hood and his Merrie Men. However the image of the man in such colours was also associated with woodsmen, foresters, etc., who were important figures in the locality for they managed the woodland.

Loose

Derived from Old English *hlose*, and indeed listed as Hlose in the eleventh century, this name tells us it was the '(place of) the pig sty'.

Shernfold Farm is a local name taking its name from the family of Galfridus de Sharnworth, a thirteenth century family who also appear on the map as the name of Shernfold Pond.

The place gives its name to the stream, itself the reason for the existence of the former paper making industry. Another reminder of yesteryear can be found on the hill near the Chequers public house. The steep incline meant the landlords enjoyed an income from providing horses to help haul the carts to the top of the hill. Even then the horses required rests and stones still line the road although they no longer take the weight of the load on ropes while the horses take a well-earned breather.

Luddesdown

A name which has changed little over the centuries, despite the rather different spelling seen in the tenth century record of Hludesduna and as Ledesdune in Domesday. This shows the name is from a Saxon or Jute personal name and Old English *dun* which together describes 'the hill of a man called Hlud'.

Bowman's Hill is recorded as Bawmans Hill in 1572 and as the modern form a century later, these late records showing this must be a reference to an otherwise unrecorded former landowner. From Old English *ellen sol* comes Elliston Bottom or 'the muddy pool by the elder trees'. Goldings Wood has been seen since the sixteenth century, this being an old manorial name. Hatch Hill was indeed a 'hill with a hatch or gate' leading to it and derived from *haecc hyll*. Henley Street is a reminder of a lost place name from *henn leah* 'the woodland clearing frequented by hen birds'.

The name of the Cock Inn may have indicated this was a venue for cock fighting, yet this image is also seen in heraldry and for a strange concoction called 'cock ale', which combined the boiled meat of a cockerel with ale and selected herbs and vegetables, depending on ones taste.

Lullingstone

Found as Lolingestone in Domesday, this was from a Saxon or Jute personal name and Old English *tun*, which together describe the 'farmstead of a man called Lulling'.

Great Cockerhurst is found as Cokerhirst in 1254 and as Kokerhurst in 1314, this from *cocer hyrst* and describing 'the wooded hill where wood is gathered for arrows', quite literally 'quiver hill'.

In 1939 archaeologists uncovered a Roman villa. Dated to around ad100 and some of the finest remains ever uncovered from the period, it included a Christian chapel, itself likely the earliest evidence of the followers of Christ in Britain.

Luton

First seen in a document from 1240 as Leueton, this is from a Saxon or Jute personal name and Old English *tun*. From this we can deduce this place began life as 'the farmstead of a man called Leofa'.

Settington is a local name first seen in the thirteenth century. Here the common suffix *tun* follows a Saxon personal name to speak of 'the farmstead of a woman called Sidewynn'.

CHAPTER TWELVE – M

Maidstone

From the late tenth century comes the record of Maegthan stan and as Meddestane in Domesday. This name seems to be from Old English *maegth stan* and speak of this as 'the stone of the maidens', a gathering or meeting place for reasons unknown.

East Barming and West Barming share an Old English origin of *bremel leah ingas* 'the people of the woodland clearing covered by brambles'. The additions are obvious and show there was one original settlement, the second created as an overspill. Barnet is an alternative name for Little Barming, the original name with the diminutive suffix *-et*. Bircholt is from Old English *bierce holt* 'the thicket of the birch trees'.

Blackmanstone is found in Domesday as Blachemenestone, showing this to be 'the farmstead of a man called Blaecman'. However we should also note the Domesday record may be misleading and this is not a personal name but a nickname, thus this would be seen as 'the farmstead of the dark-faced one'. Felderland is recorded as Feldwareland in 1226, this telling it was 'the agricultural land of the Feldware tribe'. Recorded as Greneburgh in 1375, Greenborough Marshes began as *grene beorg* 'the green mound or barrow' with the wetland reference superfluous as the area was mainly marsh.

Bletchingley is recorded in 1334 as Blecchelegh, this describes 'the woodland clearing of a man called Bleccan'. Found as Burnlegh in 1240, Boarley is a corruption of *burna leah* or 'the woodland clearing with a stream running through it'. Chesley is recorded as Chacheleye in 1270, from a Saxon or Jute personal name and Old English *leah* this is 'the woodland clearing of a man called Caecca'. In Willington Road and Willington Green we find an old place name recorded since at least the thirteenth century, the name describing 'the farmstead associated with a man called Wilde'.

Dean Street is recorded in 1324 as Denestrete and telling of 'the narrow road in the valley' from Middle English *dene strete*. Fairlawn is seen since the seventeenth century, first as Fayrelane and later as Fair Lane. The modern suffix -lawn appears to be a corruption and points to 'the lane used by and to reach the fair'. Upper Fant appears as simply Fant in 1782, this describing 'the place of ferns', the addition is to distinguish this from Frant (which has identical origins) in neighbouring Sussex.

From Old English *geoc* comes the measure of land seen in the name of Half Yoke. While most of the country used the hide, the sulung was peculiar to Kent and the yoke was a quarter of a sulung. The hide was not a specific size, simply that amount of land required to feed one family for one year. Although the hide is often quoted as equal to 120 acres, this is simply the average for the area which can vary wildly depending upon the soil, the size of the family, the climate, and the ability of the farmer. An average sulung was roughly half a hide, while a yoke was a quarter of sulug, and thus the average yoke was approximately 15 acres.

Friningham, found as Ferningeham in 1086 and as Freningham in 1206 probably refers to 'the homestead of the dwellers of or by the ferns'. Garrington is an old name found as Warwintone in Domesday, this tells of 'the *tun* or farmstead of a woman called Garwynn'. Harbourland Close neither is nor has it ever been a conduit to the open ocean. Here is a name found as Hereburglond in 1313 and one referring to 'the agricultural land of a woman called Hereburh'. Penenden Heath features the suffix *denn* and describes 'the woodland pasture of a man called Pinna', with the earliest record that of Pinnedennam in Domesday.

Early records of Hartridge, such as Hatherugg in 1292 and Hartheregge in 1327, is derived from *harath hrycg* or 'the wooded ridge', a name which still describes the region in the twentieth century. Murrain Wood appeared as Moriene in 1226, this from Middle English *moryne* meaning 'disease, plague'. It is unlikely this should be taken literally, more likely this should be viewed as a derogatory name aimed at those in residence. Woodcut is seen as Wodecote in 1327, a name from Old English *wudu cot* and talking of 'the cottage in a wood'.

Pickering Street remembers former residents, although as they were here before 1327 their name is found as Pikynge, Pykynge and Pykyngges. Plaistow

Square features is a common modern place name derived from Old English *pleg stow* to tell of 'the place of play'. Provender Way can be traced to late thirteenth century, when the family of John de Provender were landholders. Runham Lane is derived from *rum hamm* for it speaks of 'the wide water meadow', the first element literally 'roomy'. Westenhanger has many records dating back from the twelfth century, this featuring a Saxon tribal name in 'the *hangar* or wooded slope of the Osteringas'. This tribal name speaks of them as 'the knotty or lumpy ones'.

Sandling appears as Sandlinke in 1293 and as Sandlyng in 1466. This represents Old English *sand hlinc* and speaks of 'the sandy soil of the rising ground'. Thornhill Farm remains as clear today as it did when seen exactly as it appears today in a fourteenth century document, this is 'the hill marked by thorn bushes' from Old English *thorn hyll*. Tovil, found as Tobbeffeld in 1218, is from Old English *toh feld* or 'the tough open land', understood as being hard to work. The new of Maplesden comes from *mapuldre treowes denn* or 'the woodland pasture by the maple trees'.

For what seem an interesting name Ye Olde Thirsty Pig has no etymological story to tell as it was only coined in the 1990s. However it does show how a good name can attract interest. The reverse is the case with the Flower Pot, for what seems a simple reference to a decorative display has an interesting history (even if this may not be the actual origin here). Flowers were suddenly unpopular as pub names when the Puritans dominated the country following the execution of Charles I. This was down to the flowers being used to represent saints, particularly the lily and the Virgin Mary, and Puritans disliked saints and symbolism so these disappeared. However pubs named the Flower Pot suddenly appeared at this time, alluding to the flower and thus the saint.

Another seemingly religious reference is seen in the Druids Arms, the priesthood of the Celts so despised by the Romans who eradicated them. However this is misleading, for the real reference is to the United Ancient Order of Druids and showing such met within. Ironically this friendly society, despite its name, was only founded in 1781, at least two millennia after the originals. In the Rifle Volunteers we find a reference to the soldiers who were so keen to serve their country they were not only required to purchase their own rifle but also arrange tuition in marksmanship before being allowed to join up. The Dragoon public house gets its name from the soldiers, originally a nickname from a corruption of 'dragon' telling of them spitting fire from their fire-arms.

At the Old House at Home the name remembers a ballad popular with soldiers serving abroad. It was the title of an old ballad, one which speaks of a mother and her son, both remembering how content both were in earlier times. The Holly Bush is a variation on the very old sign of the bush, itself used to advertise an ale house. Another 'tree' name is found in the Old Beech Inn, where the great antiquity is more likely to have been applied to the tree before the inn.

John Churchill earned himself a reputation as a skilled statesman and brilliant soldier. In his career he ended the rebellion of the Duke of Monmouth and was instrumental in winning victories during the War of Spanish Succession. A nation and monarch presented him with the estate and house of Blenheim Palace, also giving him the title which now appears in the pub name of the Duke of Marlborough. That monarch is remembered by the Queen Anne public house.

The Chiltern Hundreds pub gets its name from an area of land owned by the Crown. When any member of parliament wishes to resign he or she applies for stewardship of the Chiltern Hundreds, the conflict of interests bar an MP from holding both and the resignation is a foregone conclusion. The Malta Inn remembers the bravery of the islanders who awarded the George Cross having been bombed mercilessly for some three years. However this is not the origin of the name that was much earlier when it became a crown colony in the early nineteenth century.

The Papermakers Arms speaks for itself, although this describes the earliest method of making paper rather than the commercial method. Another trade gave a name to the Fisherman's Arms. In the British Queen the reference is to Boudica, queen of the Celtic Iceni tribe. At the Redstart is a pub named after the bird, itself named from the Old English *red steort* which describes 'the red tail' there for everyone to see. In the Duke of Edinburgh we have a pub named after the second son of Queen Victoria. He was the first member of the royal family to set foot in Australia but may have wished he had stayed at home when wounded by a would-be assassin.

Malling (East & West)

Records of the basic name include Meallingas in 942 and as Mellingetes in 1086, the additions require no explanation. Here a Saxon or Jute personal name combines with Old English *ingas* and describes the '(place of) the family or followers of a man called Mealla'.

Blacklands is found as the hamlet Blaklond in 1392, this describes itself quite well. A reference to a tributary of the Medway is seen in Broadwater Farm, a warning it will prove difficult to cross. Swan Street was named for being home to the family of Thomas le Swon. Well Street is recorded as Ewelle in 1240, this from *ae wielle* and talking of it being 'at the well'.

The Lobster Pot may seem an odd pub name in West Malling for the sea is a long way from here. With the addition of 'pot' this most likely points to the earlier livelihood of a former landlord. Yet there is still the temptation to point to 'lobster' being used in the seventeenth century as an insult aimed at Parliamentarian soldiers. At the King and Queen the pub, on land which came to the Crown in 1539, has been under the control of both kings and queens ever since.

Many families chose the bear as the image on their coat of arms, hence the number of oddly coloured ursine images on pubs but here it is simply the Bear. 15 September 1940 was the date of the Battle of Britain, a pivotal day during the Second World War and epitomised by the aircraft seen in the name of the Spitfire public house. The Joiners Arms is a reference to one of the major skills in the building trade, along with carpentry and masons.

Marden

Listed as Maeredaen around the end of the eleventh century, this name comes from Old English *maere denn* and describes the 'woodland pasture for mares'.

To the east is the hamlet of Claygate, from *claeg geat* this literally is 'the way to the clayey land'. Here is Bockingfold, or 'the *falod* or fold of the family or followers of a man called Bocca'. Bogden also features a Saxon personal name with an Old English suffix, here *denn* tells of 'the woodland pasture of a man called Bucge'. Both Great Cheveney and Little Cheveney share an origin in 'the dry ground in a marsh of a man called Ceofa'. Silver Locks can be traced to 1473 and the family of Agnes Silverlock. In Turkey Farm we have a reminder of former resident John Turke, a man who is highly unlikely to have even heard of a turkey let alone seen one.

Collier street sign

Records include Cheuenay in 1254, Chiuneneye in 1261, Chyvene in 1308, and Chevene in 1309, the location of Great Cheveney would suggest this was the original settlement while Little Cheveney was founded as a satellite community. Collier Street can be traced to a document dated 1348, when the family of William Collier were here. Haviker Street appears as Hauekere in the thirteenth century, a name from Old English *heaford aecer* 'the agricultural land on the headland'. Curtisden Green is a Middle English name referring to the *denne* or pasture of the family of John Curteys', recorded here in 1292.

Collier Street Church of St Margaret

Horlands is a late change for earlier this was Horherst, a name from 'the filthy wooded hill' which has become 'the filthy agricultural land'. Early records of Hurstfield Farm show this to be from 'the *feld* or open land of a man called Herebeorht'. Other 'wood' names inspired Marden Beech and Marden Thorn, which are named after those respective trees. Moatlands describes itself as having 'a moat', a defensive ditch. Widehurst Farm and Widehurst Road are derived from the suffix *hyrst* and a Saxon personal name giving 'the wooded hill of a woman called Wiggyth'.

From Old English *meres eg* comes a name recorded as Mereseye in 1278 and found as Murzie Farm on today's maps. The Old English origin describes its location as 'the island in the pool'. Great Pattenden and Little Pattenden share a common origin from a Saxon personal name and the suffix *denn* and refer to 'the woodland pasture of a man called Peata'. Underling Green is derived from *under denne* and refers to this place as 'below the pastureland'. Wanshurst Green appears as Wendeshase and Wondeshese in the thirteenth century, this from *haes* and a Saxon personal name 'the place covered with brushwood of a man called Wand'.

Pub names include the Unicorn, a name which is undoubtedly heraldic but the problem is in knowing its origins. The Worshipful Company of Wax Chandlers, the Worshipful Company of Apothecaries, the Worshipful Company of Goldsmiths, all include a unicorn in their arms but the most likely origin is Scotland, the arms brought here with unification with England. The Wild Duck refers to this region being a habitat for wild birds.

Matfield

Listed as Mattefeld around 1230, this features a Saxon or Jute personal name and Old English *feld* which together speak of 'the open land of a man called Matta'.

Ashmere is found as Assem'e in 1292, coming from *aesc mere* 'the pool by the ash trees'. The name of Kippings Cross is derived from the family of William and Thomas Kypping, here in the early sixteenth century. Petteridge Lane has a name first seen in 747 as Paetlanhyrge, with the suffix *hrycg* following a Jute or Saxon personal name and speaking of 'the ridge of a man called Paetla'.

Pub names include the Star Inn, a name clearly showing a link to the church and most often through the land belonging to the second largest landholder in the country. The Hopbine refers to the hops which are used in brewing but, in order to stand out from others in the centre famous for its hop-growing, chose to refer to the plant on which the hops grow. This makes more sense as we are more likely to recognise the plant trained along the wires than a few hops on their own.

In the Wheelwrights Arms the sign carries the coat of arms of the Worshipful Company of Wheelwrights, an indication the premises could work on the waggons as well as offer stabling and refreshment for the traveller. Specific travellers gave a name to the Blue Boys Inn, for this was where George IV stopped to have the horses of his company shod. With his attendants wearing coats and headgear of blue, the name was changed to mark this auspicious occasion.

Medway (River)

The earliest surviving record may date from the eighth century where it appears as Medeuuaege, however the name is from a much era period. This seems to be a combination of the Celtic river name Wey, a name of obscure etymology, and Celtic or Old English *medu* meaning 'mead' and a description of the water, either its colour or sweetness.

Unlike place names, almost always a description of the local area, rivers and streams are not isolated in one particular area. For example there are three rivers called the Derwent in the land, the name describing the oak trees along the banks. With almost two hundred miles of banks there can never have been oak trees growing along every mile for the landscape simply could not sustain these massive trees.

All rivers age, a young vibrant and fast flowing stream, slows and meanders through lowlands, before emptying into a larger river or the sea where it may be difficult to see any movement whatsoever. When river names reflect

the nature of the river – in its simplest form the 'white river' is the young turbulent bubbling stream, while the 'dark one' is the older version with silted or muddy depths – it is clear the same name cannot be applied to the same river. However few rivers have more than one name today, while historically, when people would be unlikely to see more than the one sizable river in their entire lives, finding the name of the river depended upon where and whom the question was asked. One tributary of the Medway is a good example for alternative names only fell out of favour quite recently.

The modern River Bourne comes from *burna* a highly simplistic name meaning simply 'stream'. Yet as recently as the eighteenth century no less than four alternative names, from two different origins, are documented: the Busty or Buster refers to the tendency of the river to flood, while the Sheet or Shode comes from *shode* 'the branch of a river' and thus describing it as a tributary of the Medway. Here we see three origins describing three sections of the Bourne - *burna* when it was young and a mere stream; Buster in middle age when it crosses a floodplain; and *shode* at its confluence with the Medway. The Bradbourne is another tributary, one which is easily seen as 'the broad stream'.

Opposite page: The River Medway at Ashurst is the border between Kent and neighbouring Sussex

Meopham

Listed as Meapaham in 788 and as Mepeham in 1086, this name comes from a Saxon or Jute personal name and Old English *ham* which refers to 'the homestead of a man called Meapa'.

Admers Wood was recorded as Edmeris field in 1381, the field or *feld* having been superceded by the woodland but the name should be stated as 'the open land of a man called Eadmaere'. In 1348 the Blondel family were recorded living near a *scaga* or 'copse', this is today known as Blundells Shaw. Boughurst Street is documented from the twelfth century, describes 'the *hyrst* or wooded hill of a woman called Bucge'.

Camer is a very difficult name for the only early form seems quite different as Borstalle in 1381. This early name is 'the *steall* or cattle stall of a man called Bor'. It is possible the first element is from *bur* or 'bower', the Old French equivalent would be *chambre* and thus a link between the two. David Street derives its name from the family of Richard and Godfrey Dauy (Davy), recorded here in 1327.

Dedmar Hill was recorded as Duddeme in 1240 and as Dodemer in 1270. Here the Saxon or Jute personal name precedes Old English *mere* and speaks of 'the pool of a man called Dudda'. Gold Street is a narrow road on land once associated with a family called Goldyng, the name seen as Goldyngestreete in 1460. Huntingfield features Old English *inga feld* and refers to 'the open land of the family or followers of a man called Hunta'. Skinners Hill derives its name from the family of William Skynnere, who were here by the fourteenth century.

Lomer Farm took the name of former owner Richard de Lom'e, here by 1258. Melliker comes from Old English *aet thaem mildan aecere* speaking of it being 'at the cultivated land of soft soil', meaning it was easily worked. Merry Hill took the name of former occupant William le Myrye, here by 1270. Priestwood is found as Prestewude in 1240, from *preosta wudu* or 'the wood associated with the priests'.

Mereworth

A name which seems to tell of the 'enclosure of a man called Maera', where the Saxon or Jute personal name is suffixed by Old English *worth*. The name is recorded as Meranworth in 843 and as Marobrde in Domesday in 1086.

Highlands is from *heah land* and is indeed higher land, although the correct meaning is 'higher agricultural land'. Moorcocks was brought here as a surname, the family of John, Ralph, Richard, and William Morcok were first recorded here in a document dated 1320. Brewer's Hall is derived from the family named Brewer who were here until the late fifteenth century. Hawkridge is found as Hokeregge in a document dated 1256, this from Old English *hoc hrycg* or 'the ridge with a hook or spur of land'.

Mottingham

The earliest surviving record of this name comes from a document dated 1044 as Modingeham, showing this to be from Old English *ing ham* following a Saxon personal name or 'the homestead associated with a man called Moda'.

CHAPTER THIRTEEN – N

Nettlestead

Records include as Netelamstyde in the ninth century and as Nedestede in Domesday, this name comes from Old English *netele ham stede* and speaks of 'the homestead where nettles grow'.

Locally we find Cronk's Farm, a name recorded as Crangabyrum in 801, Crangabyras in 811, Cronkesbery in 1185, and Craunkebiry in 1336. This name describes 'the *byras* or hovels of the tribe called Crangas', the tribal name itself derived from 'dwellers at the bend'. The record of 1336 also describes this place as Aqua de Craunkebiry or 'the water of Craunkebiry', a reference to the stream which flows past here and forms a sharp ninety degree bend, which also tells how the tribe got their name. Hunt Street took the name of the family of Richard Hunt, documented here in 1623. Milbay's Wood has proven difficult to define, the best explanation offered suggests it comes from Mildmay, the family name of the Earl of Westmorland.

Pub names begin with the Hop Pole Inn. A famous sight in the Garden of England known for its hop picking, the name coined to advertise the product through one of its most important ingredients. A sight of local interest is seen in the windows of the church. The stained glass was, for its day, a marvellous sight to behold. This is the work of Reginald de Pympe and his son John. Together they raised the standards of stained glass in England after Reginald saw the work being done on the Continent. It is thought much of what Reginald saw was during his time in France when he is believed to have fought at Agincourt.

Northfleet

Listed as simply Flyte in the tenth century when the name came from Old English *fleot* or 'stream', by the time of Domesday this had become Norfluet or 'the northern stream'. The addition distinguishes this from Southfleet.

Shears Green is first seen in documents from the fourteenth century, when records show this to be from *scirgerefa grene* or 'the estate of the sheriff'. Pepper Hill was earlier recorded as Pepperness, itself derived from *pipor naess* and telling of 'the headland with soil resembling peppercorn'. This name has been recorded since 1023 and only became 'hill' comparatively recently.

September 1940 is remembered as a major turning point of the Second World War. Described by Winston Churchill as 'the few', the pilots of the Royal Air Force battled the enemy in the skies above Kent. This victory was seen as turning the tide and preventing invasion. With the county being at the forefront of this confrontation it was inevitable public houses would be named the Battle of Britain, as is the local at Northfleet.

Almost a year after the Battle of Britain, on Friday 16 August 1941, some 150 German aircraft flew over Kent, unleashing their payloads over several places in the area. Northfleet suffered greatly that day, with a total of 106 bombs dropped, ranging from 100 to 500 pounds. Next day Northfleet counted 29 dead and 27 injured.

It may seem an odd choice to name a pub after a type of tea, but actually both are named after another politician and former prime minister. The Earl Grey remembers Charles Grey, the second to hold the title, who is best remembered for his support in the abolition of the slave trade.

North Ockendon

Seen as Wokendune in the late eleventh century and as Wochenduna in Domesday, this is 'the hill of a man called Wocca' where the Saxon personal name is suffixed by Old English *dun*. The addition of North distinguishes this from South Ockendon.

CHAPTER FOURTEEN – O

Offham

Derived from a Saxon or Jute personal name and Old English *ham*, this name tells us it was 'the homestead of a man called Offa'. The name is first seen as Offaham in the tenth century.

Aldon, found as Aledon in 1240, is a reminder of 'the hill of a man called Aella'. Great Comp and Little Comp appear as Compe in 1461, this from Old English *camp* or 'field'.

Locals drinking at the Kings Arms may once have been convinced to frequent this bar, instead of the competition, through it advertising itself as a patriotic establishment.

The village green still has its quintain, thought to be the last surviving example of such *in situ* in the country. A quintain is a post around eight feet in height with a single arm extending equally both sides, making it look for all the world like an ordinary fingerpost. However closer inspection shows this arm rotates freely and forms the equipment used in a sport popular in medieval times across Europe and probably beyond. On one end a heavy object, commonly a leather pack, was hung with the opposite arm, or eye, being the target. A rider would attempt to hit the target with his lance, yet this was not as simple as it sounds for a good speed was required otherwise the arm would swing around and the weight knock him unceremoniously from his saddle.

Oldbury

Listed as Ealdebery in 1302, this name comes from Old English *eald burh* and describes 'the old stronghold'. An old stronghold but a 120 acre site which has not been occupied since 50bc. Archaeological evidence has shown this place was burned and abandoned, perhaps as a result of one of the raids on Britain by the Romans under Julius Caesar almost a century before the Empire arrived to stay.

Orpington

Seen as Orpedingtun in 1032 and as Orpington for the first time in the Domesday record of 1086. Here a Saxon personal name precedes Old English *ing tun* and refers to 'the farmstead associated with a man called Orped'.

The local name of Kevington has changed little since its earliest record as Keuington in 1610, the modern form found for the first time just eighty years later. This comes from Old English *cyfing tun* meaning 'the farmstead of the tub', this refers to a mound which, with a little imagination, may be described as tub-shaped. Both Petleys and Lower Petleys, the addition is self-explanatory, are recorded since the fourteenth century. From Old English *pytt leah* this tells of 'the woodland clearing where a pit can be seen'.

St Mary Cray takes its name from the river and the dedication of the church. The river name is of Celtic or British derivation meaning 'the fresh or clean one'. St Paul's Cray is another example, the place recorded as simply Craie in the Domesday record of 1086. Tubbenden appears as Tubindenn in 1240 and as Tubbingden in 1309, this featuring a Saxon personal name and the suffix *denn* and telling of 'the woodland pasture of a man called Tubba'. Both Gumping Road and Gumping Common are recorded as Gunnepende in 1479, this describing 'the pound or enclosure of a man called Gunna'.

Among the most common pub names in the country is the Royal Oak, indeed there are more than twenty-five in Kent alone. This comes as no surprise for it recalls one of the most famous events in English history. September 1651 and following defeat at the Battle of Worcester Charles II and his aide, Colonel Carless, flee the scene. In hot pursuit are several enemy soldiers who chase them to Boscobel House at Shifnal in Shropshire, where the Penderel brothers were known supporters of the king. Too risky to hide in the house, the two men took to the branches of an oak tree in the grounds where, unbeknown to the soldiers who walked just feet below them, they remained in the branches until it was safe to descend.

Eventually, after a long and dangerous journey aided by the Penderel brothers, the king escaped to the Continent. The oak tree itself survived for many years, although it suffered greatly during the Victorian era from those looking for a memento of their visit. Today seedlings are sold, these are advertised as certified grandsons of the original Boscobel Oak and remain in great demand. Back in the seventeenth century and the eventual Restoration of the Monarchy, the episode in the tree was recalled when the king's birthday, 29 May, was declared Royal Oak Day. This remained a public holiday until quite recently. Children would dress in oak leaves to celebrate the return of the monarch, while those who were not suitably attired were looked upon as being anti-royalist and, children or not, were thrashed with bunches of nettles carried specifically for the purpose.

Another common pub name is the Blacksmiths Arms, one which dates from the days when the pub and the village metalworker provided the same service for the rider and his horse as the motorway service station does for a driver and his vehicle today. Advertising is also seen in the name of the Bottle and Jug, this time the beer is being promoted. Another invitation, this time specifically after dark, is offered at the Harvest Moon, this being the name given to an autumn full moon which gives the longest hours of moonlight. At the Rose and Crown symbols representing the nation and the monarchy is an indication of a patriotic establishment.

Orpington is probably best known for giving its name to a breed of chicken. There are several colours, one of which has given a name to the Buff public house. That this colour has been chosen, rather than the blue or black, is probably because of the slang term 'buff' used to mean 'attractive'.

Otford

Listed as Otteford in 832 and as Otefort in the Domesday record of 1086, this comes from a Saxon or Jute personal name and Old English *ford* and speaks of 'the ford of a man called Otta'.

Otford Village

Romney Street most likely derives its name from the family of Roger Romeyn, living near the *straet* or Roman road by 1327. Twitton comes from *thwit tun* and tells of 'the farmstead in a detached area', a barrier created by the adjacent marshland. Horns Green is derived from *horn* and refers to 'the projection of land' and recorded as Horne in 1292.

Otford street Sign

One local pub is called the Horns, a name advertising the product as the draymen would announce their imminent arrival by sounding a horn.

Otham

Domesday records this name as Oteham in 1086, this Domesday record shows this to be a Saxon or Jute personal name and Old English *ham* and telling us this was 'the homestead of a man called Otta'.

The local name of Stoneacre almost speaks for itself as 'the stony cultivated land'.

CHAPTER FIFTEEN – P

Paddock Wood

It is still easy to see this place name as meaning 'the small enclosure, paddock', the name is derived from Old English *pearroc* and recorded as Parrok in 1279.

Badsell is found as Badeshull in 1227, this is 'the *syle* or miry place of a man called Beada'. Eastlands is easy to see as 'the land east of the parish'. Mascalls has been recorded as a place name since the late fifteenth century, although the origin is some years older as it comes from the family of Agnes Mascalle who were here by 1327. Found as Oueney in 1313, Oveny Green is from *ufan eg* and pointing out this settlement is found 'on the island'.

Tollhurst is derived from Old English *tunlafe hyrst* or 'the wooded hill associated with the heirs'. Tatlingbury is first seen in 1206 as Tetlingebir, this featuring the suffix *burh* with a Saxon personal name and telling of 'the stronghold of a man called Taetel'. Whetstead appears as Hwaetanstede and as Hwetenstede in the ninth century, this from *hwaeten stede* and speaking of 'the place where wheat is grown'. Courthopes Corner is derived from Middle English *curt hop* or 'the short valley'.

Once known as the Kent Arms, the John Brunt VC is the only pub ever named after a recipient of the Victoria Cross. John Brunt spent his formative years in Paddock Wood where he was known as a daring, mischevious and yet caring individual and this stayed with him throughout his military career. Following action in North Africa he landed in Italy and was given command of a platoon. In December 1943 Lieutenant Brunt, with his platoon under heavy bombardment, crossed the river so many times in order to retrieve the wounded the men called the river Brunt's Brook and he was subsequently awarded the Military Cross. Injury saw him sent back to Africa to recover, but soon returned to Italy where he rallied his men time and again to take the enemy's hold in the town where they were outnumbered by three to one. Under intense fire he sat on the turret of a Sherman tank and went from one position to another, rescuing his wounded and killing a great number of the enemy. His leadership, bravery and devotion to duty were beyond praiseworthy and would earn him the highest award bestowable in the British armed forces. Sadly he never received the award as John Brunt was killed by mortar fire next day.

Paddock Wood may have been an equally dangerous place to live in August 1896, for it is on record as the scene of the first speeding offence in Britain – or perhaps that should be the first where the driver was actually charged. When the speed limit in the village was just two mph, one Walter Arnold came roaring through at an unprecedented four times the speed limit. The local constabulary chased him down, bizarrely on his bicycle, and the driver was later found guilty and fined one shilling (5p).

Peckham (East & West)

The basic name is recorded as Peccham in the tenth century and as Peche-ham in Domesday. This comes from Old English *peac ham* and describes 'the homestead by a peak or hill'.

Beltring is listed as Beltringe in 1309, this telling of the '(place of) the people of a man called Belt'. Branbridges refers to a crossing of the nearby Medway, from Old English *brant brycg* warning of 'the steep bridge. Stilstead House speaks of itself as 'the place of the thicket' from Old English *thyfel stede*.

Strettit House was built on an area previously recorded as Strodettcrosse in 1404, this telling of 'the marshy ground covered with brushwood' and having now lost all reference to a marker or crossroads. Albans is derived from a former lord of the manor, one Alban de Wandsworth associated with this place from 1305. Barnes Street describes itself as 'the dweller by the barn'. Pub names include the Man of Kent, a traditional term used to describe a man born in Kent to the east of the Medway.

East Peckham has often been said to have moved from an original site much closer to Mereworth. Yet while the church of St Michael's is found a couple of miles from the village, there is no evidence to suggest this has ever been the case.

Pembury

A name recorded as Peppingeneria at the end of the eleventh century, this name comes from a Saxon or Jute personal name and Old English *inga burh* and describes 'the fortified place of the family or followers of a man called Pepa'.

Pembury's simpler sign ....

..... and a more ornate one showing it was an important coaching stop

Amhurst Hill is from *hamm hyrst* the wooded hill by the hemmed-in land', the addition of 'Hill' is quite modern. Listed as Dudingburie in 1191, Downingbury describes itself as 'the *burh* or fortified place associated with a man called Dudda'. Fletcher's Green is, not surprisingly, associated with the family of Thomas Ffleccher, known to be here by 1354. Both Hawkwell Place and Little Hawkwell share an origin in Old English *heafoc wielle* and 'the spring or stream frequented by hawks'. Dundle Road is recorded as Derondalle in 1563, this being from Old English *dierne dael* and telling it was 'the secret or hidden valley'.

Hepsbrook Wood is a name transferred from Penshurst. However the original Hepsbrook, which described 'the marshy ground formed by a hook of land (between two streams)', is now lost. From Old English *peru steap* and recorded as Parstepe in 1270, this tells of its location 'at the pear tree on the steep place'. Rankham Wood grows in lower ground, the name confirming this as 'the valley frequented by ravens' and from Old English *hraefn cumb*. Rowley Hill is first recorded in 1313 as Raule, this being from Old English *raw leah* or 'woodland clearing with a row of dwellings'. Bopeep is an unusual name, one also found in neighbouring Sussex, and thought to refer to a look-out point or turnpike gate. Named after the monarch known as the Sailor King, the King William IV public house may well have been suggested by another with a maritime background, while the Camden Arms takes the name of a local family.

The Camden Arms at Pembury

In the early twentieth century Pembury became the location for a new hospital, one where cutting edge technology was employed to research and treat the problems associated with the outbreak of hodophobia. Never before had cases been reported of this condition and no wonder, for until the introduction of the motor car nobody could have a phobia related to such travel. Several of those who came here to act as guinea pigs stayed on and their descendants still live in the parish to this day.

Penshurst

Found as Penshurst in 1072, this name comes from Old English *hyrst* with a Saxon or Jute personal name and tells us of 'the wooded hill of a man called Pefen'.

Penshurst's village sign

Hartsland was an area held by John Hert, a husbandman of Penshurst, by 1450. What began as Lancup Well and now seen as Lancup Lake, is not recorded until the fifteenth century and if this is, as it seems, an old stream name the forms are far too late to give it as anything but 'the stream named Lan or Lanne'. Redleaf House took the name of the estate, itself named from the different foliage which was of a reddish hue at times of the year other than autumn. Russell's Wood takes the name of Simon and William Russel who were working this land by 1278. Salmans Lane is another from a former resident, this time it is 1313 and the family of Thomas Salamon. Elliot's Farm takes its name from former resident Richard Elyot, here in 1327. Ford Place is simple enough and means exactly what it says.

At the Leicester Arms the sign depicts an image of Robert Dudley, Earl of Leicester. He is connected to the village through his appointment as Baron Penshurst on the accession of James I of England and VI of Scotland. Of course he was also said to be the long-time lover of Queen Elizabeth I, it is rumoured many of their trysts saw them meet at Penshurst. A less obvious name is that of the Spotted Dog, for the image was originally referring to the coat of arms of the Sydney family and was actually three leopards. Hence the name is a critical comment on the artistic talents of the sign painter.

To complete the trio of interesting pub names we come to the Bottle House. The origin and reason for the choice of this name is depicted on the sign in the form of the verse:

From this bottle I am sure,
You'll get a glass both good and pure;
Each goodman and eke his spouse
Drink to each other and this house.

Petts Wood

A comparatively modern name which records the arrival of the Pett family by 1577. In that year this family of ship-builders were leased to take the oak from the trees growing in the wood. Not only are they remembered in the place name but also in the local pub name of the *Sovereign of the Seas*. In 1634 one Phineas Pett built this, the finest vessel of its day, for Charles I. It sailed the seas until catching fire in 1697.

When the chain of F. W. Woolworth closed in 2009, the manager of the Petts Wood branch realised he was the last to close its doors for business in the United Kingdom. What began as the germ of a ludicrous idea to benefit from the British fascination with nostalgia, he gathered together the remnants of the store's best-known range – the Pick-and-Mix at the sweet counter. What would have retailed at two to three pounds was put up at auction and realised the astonishing sum of £14,500.

Pilgrim's Way

Not only one of the most famous routes in Kent but also in the country. It is named as it is the traditional route followed by those journeying to the tomb of St Thomas a Becket in Canterbury Cathedral. It runs along the line of the North Downs between the border with neighbouring Surrey to Felixstowe, running both ways as pilgrims travel to Canterbury from both directions. However the route was in use well before the reign of Henry II and Becket, his Archbishop of Canterbury, and was a trading route in use well before the arrival of the Romans. Indeed archaeological evidence has dated this route to at least bc500 and there is every reason to believe it had been in use before either Stonehenge (2,500 bc) or even Avebury (4,000 bc) had been laid out.

The most famous road name in the county

Plaxtol

Records of this name begin with Plextole in 1386, this comes from Old English *pleg stow* and describes 'the place for play or sport'.

Locally we find Old Soar, first recorded in 1480 and derived from the family of John le Suur and Roger le Soure both here in the thirteenth century and undoubtedly of the same family despite the rather different spelling of the surname. Oxen Hoath comes from *oxa snad* and tells of 'the small area of land where oxen are reared'. The Shode is a minor river branch, it comes from Old English *sceadan* meaning 'divide, separate'. The modern name of Clearhedges Wood sounds something of an oxymoron. Yet the original name made sense as 'the agricultural land cleared of hedges', the woodland grew much later and simply took on an existing name.

As a pub name the Papermakers Arms seems to be nothing more than a trade name, and one of particular popularity in Kent. However it is also true to say landlords are well known for the subtlest of messages on their signs and, together with the humour of pub names, perhaps there is a hidden comment here. In the earliest days, when paper was made by hand, a slurry of wood fibres and water was scooped up in a wire frame and shaken to ensure the thin film was evenly distributed and thus, when allowed to dry, would produce a sheet of paper of uniform thickness. As a result the papermakers were instantly recognised because their hands would constantly shake and perhaps this is the reference to their 'arms' here.

Plumstead

Seen as Plumstede in 969 and as Plumestede in 1086, this comes from Old English *plume stede* and describes 'the place where plum trees grow'.

Between 1886 and 1913 various football grounds in the area played host to one of the most famous football clubs in the world, albeit while in their early days and then known as Royal Arsenal and then Woolwich Arsenal. Today the Arsenal have moved from their first permanent home at Highbury and now play at the Emirates Stadium.

Pratt's Bottom

A name seen for the first time in 1801, the name refers to 'the valley associated with the family of Pratt', who were known in this part of the world from at least the fourteenth century. We also find Pratt's Grove, more likely to have been transferred from Pratt's Bottom than having a shared origin.

CHAPTER SIXTEEN – R

Rainham

A place name first found in 811 when it is documented as Roegingaham. This comes from an Old English tribal name and *ham*, giving 'the homestead of the Roegingas' although the tribal name has never been defined nor understood.

Berengrave is a late name, not seen before 1782 although the form almost certainly points to an origin of *bern graefe* 'the barn by a thicket or grove' rather than *bern graef* 'the barn by a grave or trench'. Macklands is recorded as Makeland in 1291, this coming from a Saxon personal name and Old English *land* to refer to 'the farmland of a man called Maca'. Mardale House stands on land which was clearly once flooded on a regular basis for the name comes from *mere dael* 'the valley of the pool'.

Motley Hill is found as Mottene in 1270, a name from Old English *aet thaere motten eg* and telling us it was found 'at the dry land with gritty soil'. Siloam, first seen as Syleha in 1226, comes from Old English *syle hamm* and speaks of 'the miry hemmed-in area'. Stoners Rough Wood is derived from the family of Nicholas Stonhard, who was living here by 1327. From Old English *stede* and a Saxon personal name, Cowstead describes itself as 'the place of a man called Cuda'. Cozenton is seen as Cusinton in 1235, this describing 'the *tun* or farmstead of a man called Cusa'.

The Macklands Arms is a pub name coming from the premises, formerly Macklands House and home to the Mackay family. The pride in being a man or maid of Kent is seen in the naming of the Men of Kent. Concorde was a famous name in aviation history, the first supersonic jet airliner and thereafter a name of a pub in Rainham. An earlier mode of transport, the railway, contributed to the explosion of the population of Rainham which, at the census of 1801, numbered just 422 and exactly two centuries later exceeded six thousand.

Ravensbourne (River)

That this features a word from Old English *hraefn* is entirely down to the number of 'raven' names found, not only in Kent but, throughout the country. However the true origin is revealed by records of Randesbourne in 1360 and as Rendesburne in 1372, showing the modern form to be a corruption of 'the stream of a man called Rendel'.

Riverhead

A name which shows the value of finding as many early forms as possible, for without these old records this would surely be thought of as a reference to a river source. However a quick look at the record from 1278 shows this name as Reddride, a name from Old English *hrither hyth* and describing 'the landing place for cattle'.

Rochester

Found as Hrofaescaestir in 731 and as Rowecestre in 1086, this features the Old English *ceaster* and describes 'the Roman stronghold called Hrofi'. This Celtic name seems to from the same source as the fourth century record of Durobrivis, a name which refers to 'the walled town with the bridges'.

Today the word 'borstal' is known as a place for young offenders, although the term is no longer considered politically correct. This began as a place name Borstal coming from Old English *borg steall* which, ironically, describes 'place of refuge or security'. History also used the word in a quite different sense, 'borstal' was once a common dialect word referring to 'a steep, narrow path worn on the sides of hills'. Clearly this last sense must have a quite different etymology.

Bully Hill is a name from Old French *boulaie*, recorded as Boley in 1278, Boleye in 1338, Bullyhill in 1442, and The Bullie in 1460, it describes 'the place covered with birch trees'. Delce is recorded as such in Domesday in 1086, from *dalas* it refers to 'doles, divisions' (of land). Nashenden Farm has a name which began as Hyscen in 995 with a name referring to 'the boundary place of the small house of the pasture' and evolved to describe 'a woodland pasture marked by a small house'. Both are not only similar but also probably correct for all boundaries inland are movable.

Pattens Lane comes from the thirteenth century, by which time it was home to the family of one Benjamin Petyn, the surname also given as Potyn. Upnor is first seen in 1292 as Nore, this from *atten ore* and meaning 'at the bank'. Later the name changed to describe it as 'upon the bank', thus Upnor's name came about when the castle was built here. Prior to that the name referred to the bank and not the building standing there.

The Nags Head is among the most common of pub names. While the term 'nag' is today used in a derogatory sense, when it first appeared as a pub name it referred to a sturdy horse available for hire by travellers. Ridden from here to the next establishment in the chain the horses remained comparatively fresh, cutting journey times significantly. For ladies who consider the alternative use of 'nag' unacceptable, they might be interested to learn it was only ever used for males until quite recently.

The location of the county as a first line of defence against invasion has been recalled in pub names such as the City Walls, also indicating its location, and the Norman Conquest. Advertising a trade is a favourite for names with landlords. In the Coopers Arms we find the trade name of the barrel makers, which also hints at the product. When it comes to history we cannot ignore the association between this area and one of our best-loved writers, Rochester having a Dickens Festival twice every year. Several pubs have been named from his titles, the *David Copperfield* just one example, but surely the best is the What The Dickens, which also doubles as an expression meaning "Goodness me!" On the subject of expressions, another pub name exhibits mild surprise in the Who'd A Thought It.

Ryarsh

Domesday lists this as Riesce in 1086, later found as Rierssh in 1242. Here the name is derived from Old English *ryge ersc* and refers to 'the ploughed field used for growing rye'.

The local name of Calais Court is documented as 'Carews Court, now commonly called Callis Court' in a document dated 1782. This shows how the modern name has been further corrupted, doubtless influenced by other places named 'Calais' in Kent, from the original referring to the Carew family who came here in 1433. Engeham is recorded as Eadinghame in 1278 and as Edyngeham in 1313, this coming from Old English *ing ham* following a Saxon personal name as 'the homestead associated with a man called Eadda'.

Here one pub is named after Arthur Wellesley, better known by his title of Duke of Wellington which is how he is known here. His most famous act was to lead the forces to defeat the French at the Battle of Waterloo, however thereafter he went on to have a very successful political career.

CHAPTER SEVENTEEN – S

Seal

Seen in the Domesday survey as La Sela, this comes from Old English *sele* and refers to 'the hall or dwelling'.

Seal village sign

Bitchet Green, Bitchet Common, and Lower Bitchet share a name brought here by the family de la Birchette in the thirteenth century, their surname meaning 'the dwellers by the birch trees'. Broadoak is a common name, one coming from *brad ac* and describing the marker known as 'the broad oak'. Ducks Grove is a lasting reminder of John Ducke, resident here in 1278.

Sevenoaks

Listed as Seouenaca at the end of the eleventh century, this name comes from Old English *seofon ac* and describes the '(place by) the seven oak trees'. Famously the hurricane of October 1987 actually brought down five of these trees and, for a time at least, the place did not live up to its name.

Bayley's Hill takes its name from the family of Robert Bayly, who were recorded here in a document of 1313. Blackhall speaks for itself, a large house constructed of particularly dark materials. Brattles is recorded as Bratillys Hill in 1546, the name referring to the family found here from the fourteenth century variously named as Bratel, Bratill or Bratyll. Dibden, seen as Depedene in 1270, comes from *deop denu* the '(place at) the deep valley'. Yaldham is seen as Ealdeham in 1177, this from *ham* and a Saxon personal name describing 'the homestead of a man called Ealda'. St Julians began as a region where the Julyan family lived.

In the west of Sevenoaks we find an old place name, Edenhurst referring to 'the *hurst* or wooded hill overlooking the River Eden'. Fig Street remembers the family of Alan Ffyk, recorded here around the end of the thirteenth century. In 1327 John Godwyne was at Godden Green. First seen in 821 as Gretaniarse Greatnearse, the name of Greatness is from Old English *aet thaem greoten ersce*, telling us it was located 'at the gravelly stubble field'. Listed as Wykherst in 1292, Wickhurst comes from *wic hyrst* and describes 'the wooded hill by a specialised farm', that speciality most often dairy produce.

Hubbard's Hill, regarded since the thirteenth century, comes from Old English *hug borde* 'the side of the hill'. Knole comes from Old English *cnoll* and describes 'a hillock'. Oakwood Farm speaks of 'the oak tree wood' from Old English *ac wudu* and listed as Okwode in 1387. Panthurst has records of Paunthurst in 1407 and as Pantiers in 1455. It seems likely this is not the original name but was original known as just *hyrst* or 'wooded hill', with the later addition of the family name of Henry le Paneter who was here by 1292.

Rumshott Wood is derived from Old English *rum scydd* to tell of the 'roomy shed', the name recorded as Romesedde in 1254 and as Rumshedde in 1359. Salters Heath Farm was once home to the family of Robert the Salter, as documented in 1270. From Old English *sol feld* or 'the open land with muddy pools' comes the place name Solefield. Tanners Cross can be traced to the fourteenth century and the family named Tannere living here. Bullfinch Corner comes from a family named Bolefynch, resident here in 1348.

Shipbourne

Records of this name include Sciburna around 1100 and as Scipburn in 1198. Here the name comes from Old English *sceap burna* and describes 'the sheep stream'.

Locally we find Little Budds, recorded as Buddys in 1444 and associated with the family of Le Bud, here since at least the thirteenth century. Puttenden Manor is recorded as Puttinden in 1175, a name from *denn* with a Saxon personal name and describing 'the woodland pasture of a man called Putta'. What was once the New Inn is now the Chaser, named after the successful and popular trainer based at the nearby Fairlawne Racing Stables.

The Fairlawne Estate was home to the Vane family. During the troubled times of the English Civil War one Sir Henry Vane was a Royalist and supported Charles I. However he soon changed his allegiance to the Parliamentarians when the king was brought to trial only to revert back to his original choice on the Restoration of the Monarchy. He was executed in 1662 as, unsurprisingly, everyone considered him too dangerous to be allowed to live.

Shoreham

A name meaning 'the homestead by a steep bank or slope' which comes from Old English *scora ham*. It is recorded as Scorham in a document from 822.

Records of Filston Hall include Vieleston in 1203, Vielestone in 1212, and Vielston alias Filston in 1782. Here from Middle English *tone* with a French personal name is 'the farmstead of a man called Viel'. Listed as Goldhelle in 1332 and virtually unchanged since the original Old English *gold hyll*, Gold Hill could either refer to 'a sunny hill' or one known for a proliferation of yellow flowers at certain times of the year.

Paine's Farm dates from at least 1313, that year it was documented as home to one Richard Payn. Another farm was named for it being known as 'the sodden cut off area of ground', appearing on modern maps as Sepham Farm. Barnett's Wood gets its name from Old English *baernet* to tell us this was 'the place cleared by burning', although clearly that would have been alongside the wood.

On the May Day bank holiday each year a fund-raising event is held on the Darent. Launched at the village War Memorial, the Duck Race sees people pay a small fee to race their duck downstream in the hope the will be first past the post at the old mill.

Shorne

From Old English *scoren* and speaking of 'the steep place', this name appears as Scorene at the end of the eleventh century.

Green Farm takes its name from the family who also gave their name to Grene Manor. This in turn was built at the site of the now lost settlement of Merston, this being 'the farmstead at the marsh'. In Peartree Wood and Peartree Lane we have self-explanatory names first seen in the fourteenth century, these names based on the Old English element *pyrige*. Randle Wood is from the Old French *rondelle* to describe 'the circular wood'. Puckle Hill was clearly once the subject of a snippet of folklore for the name comes from *pucel* or 'goblin haunted'.

Sidcup

Here is a name which is first seen in a document of 1254, where it is hardly recognisable as Cetecopp. Both forms are derived from Old English *set copp* and describe 'the seat hill' and a reference to its flat summit.

Found as Blakewene in 1240, reflected in the records of Blakeben Strete and Blakeben Gate in 1407, this comes from *blaec fenn* and describes 'the dark marshland'. Lamorbey took its name from the family of Thomas Lamendby, first recorded here in 1513. Ruxley is recorded as Rochelei in the Domesday record of 1086, this from Old English *hroces leah* and referring to 'the woodland clearing frequented by rooks'. Honeyden is recorded from the eighteenth century, this from Old English *hunig den* and meaning 'the woodland pasture where hives are kept'.

When it comes to pub names the Alma Arms is named after the Battle of Alma. Fought on 20 September 1854 between the Russian forces under General Menshikov and an Anglo-French alliance commanded by Lord Raglan and General St Amaud, this is considered the first major battle of the Crimean War. Named after the nearby River Alma, the river name comes from a Crimean Tatar word for 'apple', some 3,300 of the 60,000 allied forces and 5,700 of 33,000 defeated Russians were killed in a single day.

Until methods of mining coal on an industrial basis were devised, the principal 'coal' used for fuel was charcoal. The Charcoal Burners remembers the men whose skill at cutting and slow burning roughly equal pieces of wood, covered by turfs and smouldered to remove all traces of water and impurities was to be admired. However this was nothing compared to the tedium of having to watch the mound for two, three or more days to ensure it neither burst into flames nor went out, either destroying their work. Such was the boredom of this part of the task they took to sitting on stools with just one leg, then should their eyes close they would fall from their perch and this is the origin of the phrase 'to drop off'.

The Hogshead is an advertisement for the product, this cask had no standard capacity irrespective if it contained beer or wine. At the White Cross Inn the sign shows this relates to the Knights of St John, although how the two are connected is unclear. In the Horse and Groom we find a reference to the days when the horse was the sole mode of transport overland and how the pubs would offer hospitality to both horse and rider.

Snodland

Records of this name include Snoddingland in 838 and as Esnoiland in 1086. Here a Saxon or Jute personal name and Old English *ing land* refer to 'the cultivated land associated with a man called Snodd'.

The etymology behind Crookhorn Wood is rather unusual. Dating back to the time of Domesday when one Radulfus de Curbespine was lord of the neighbouring manor of Birling. This surname, correctly Curva Spina and of obvious meaning, has been Anglicised to Crookhorn and suggests 'a crooked back'. Today only the wood carries the name suggesting it was previously considered part of the neighbouring parish. Dowde's Wood most likely takes the name of one Dud, a landowner in this area during the latter half of the tenth century.

Holborough comes from *hol beorg*, an Old English name found since the ninth century and describing 'the mound in a hollow'. Mark Farm is derived from Old English *mearc* meaning 'boundary'. Records of Povenesse in 1242, Pouenasse in 1300, Pouenesshe in 1313, and as Pawnassh in 1465 show the evolution of Punish Wood from the original *aesc* and a Saxon personal name giving 'the ash trees of a man called Pufa'. Holloway Court features a common early street name which shows just how well used it was for it describes 'the hollowed-out way', literally worn away by many years of use by feet, hooves and wheels.

At the Freemasons Arms it is not the stone workers of yesteryear who are commemorated but the fraternal society renowned for their charity work.

Southborough

Found as Borough of Suth in 1270 and as La South Burgh in 1450, this is from Old English *suth burh* and describes 'the southern borough' (in relation to Tonbridge).

Bentham Hill comes from *beonet hamm*, here understood as 'the water meadow where bent grass grows', the nearby hill taking its name from this low-lying land by the River Meadway. Berling Farm took the name of former landowner Henry de la Marche de Berling, recorded here in 1270 and whose name tells us he was 'from the boundary of Birling', that name being defined under its own entry.

Great Bounds and Little Bounds, recorded as Bounde in 1348, either tells us these were on the parish boundary or reflects a medieval surname, Le

Bounde or Le Bonde. What began as the home of John Mode in 1327, and hence known as Modes Corner, has since acquired an extra letter and given a completely different impression of the meaning of Modest Corner. Simmonds Wood takes its name from a local family, the Symonds were known to be here by 1348.

Southfleet

Documented as Suthfleotes in the tenth century and as Sudfleta in Domesday, this comes from Old English *suth fleot* and describes 'the southern place at the stream'.

Walsingham is named after the family who were lords of the manor from the fourteenth century. Scadbury Farm has changed little since first seen as Scadebery in 1327. This is understood as coming from *scaetha burh* or 'the stronghold of the thief or criminal'.

Speldhurst

Listed as Speldhirst in the eighth century, this comes from Old English *speld hyrst* and describes itself as 'the wooded hill where wood chips are found'.

Speldhurst village sign

Brackston and Breakstones share an origin, although the quarry so clearly spoken of as the place to 'break stones' in the latter example is much later than the slurred former example recorded as Brekston in 1332. Etherington Hill is recorded as Hatheregg in 1278 and as Hatheregge just twenty years later. These early forms are clearly from *haeth hrycg*, easily seen as 'the heath covered ridge', although when it acquired the suffix *tun* is not clear. Scrivington is defined as 'the farmstead associated with the family of Reginald Scroffyn', the clue found in a document dated 1292. Sherlock Cottages are a reminder of the family of Richard Shirloc, here by 1240.

Harwarton is first seen as the place name of Herewordtone in 1327, although it was earlier recorded as held by the man who gave this place its name, Thomas Hereward being here by 1292 with the rapid addition of the common element *tun*. Nellington Wood to the south is first seen as Nelehampton in 1628, named from the family of William Nelehame who were certainly here by 1240. Bullingstone has been seen since the thirteenth century, this telling of 'the farmstead of a family called Baluinch'.

An annual springtime event takes place on the second Sunday in May. While there are different age groups and categories, the Speldhurst pram race fundamentally involves a contestant pushing their 'baby' around the village a couple of times. They are compelled to visit the two drinks stations on the route every time they pass. There is no record of a single competitor ever failing to down half a pint at either of the two pubs.

Stanstead

A similar name to the previous entry, here from Old English *stan stede* and describing 'the stony place' which was recorded as Stansted in 1231.

Locally we find Rumney Farm, a name recorded since the fourteenth century and brought here by the Romeney family who must have brought the name here from Romney – this name explained as 'the roomy river'. Court Wood began as North Court in the fourteenth century, clearly being used in the sense of 'manor' and later transferred to the woodland.

Staplehurst

Appearing as Stapelhurst in 1226, this comes from Old English *stapol hyrst* and describes 'the wooded hill where posts are obtained'.

Bardingley is a name found as early as 814, the name describing 'the *leah* or woodland clearing of a man called Bearda'. Chapman Farm was worked by the family of John Chapman in 1327. Crump is a name brought here by the family of Walter Crumpe, here by 1325. Here we find a name also seen at Cobham but this example of Henhurst has a different origin. Here the records of Enghurst from 1270 and Hengherst in 1327 show this to be from *enge hyrst* and tells of 'the narrow wooded hill'. Duckhurst appears as Dokehurst in1275, showing this to be 'the *hyrst* or wooded hill of a man called Doke'. Dunbury Farm began as a settlement, this recorded as Dunningbyr in 1285 with Old English *ing burh* following a personal name to give 'the stronghold associated with a man called Dunna'.

Hobbs Wood derives its name from the family of Richard Hobbe, docu-mented as here in 1327. Featuring the suffix *denn*, Loddenden describes 'the woodland pasture of a man called Ludel'. Lovehurst Manor comes from Old English *laf hyrst* and literally describes 'the left wooded hill', telling us this is the last surviving remnant of woodland which probably formed a much larger forested area. In an area where *hyrst* seems to be the most obvious suffix, we also find 'the wooded hill near the irregularly shaped patch of ground', which has given names to Great Pagehurst and Little Pagehurst. Aydhurst is derived from *hagu thorn hyrst* and tells us this was known as 'the wooded hill where hawthorn grows'. Exhurst has changed little since the early record of Exherste, this from *aesc hyrst* 'ash tree wooded hill'.

Pile Gate, also seen in Pile Lane, is first seen in 1610 as Pylegate and may well describe a place where 'piles of wood are stacked' if this early record is around the time the name was first coined. If it is much earlier it represents Old English *pyll geat* 'the way by the pool or stream'. The earliest record of Saynden Farm dates from 830, this from *saenget denn* meaning 'the burnt woodland pasture'. Coming from Old English *snad* meaning 'a detached piece of land', this name is seen as Snode at the end of the fourteenth century and as Snoad on modern maps. Clapper Lane is seen as Clapers in 1471, this an old reference to a clapper bridge, an ancient style of footbridge where slabs of rock are supported on stone piers. Mathurst Green can only be a corruption of Bathurst, this a reminder of the charitable gift to the parish by Lancelot Bathurst in 1639. Sweetlands Corner can be traced to Old English *suth land*, 'the southern agricultural land', and was recorded as Suthland in 1278.

In 1865 a train crash at Staplehurst saw the boat train derailed while crossing the viaduct, a length of track having been removed during engineering improvements. Ten people were killed and another forty injured, although the incident is best known for the most famous passenger on board. Charles Dickens helped to tend to the injured, some of whom died. The experience affected him greatly, losing his voice for two weeks and afterwards was a bundle of nerves when travelling by train. Five years to the day after the crash Dickens died, his son later saying his father never truly recovered from the experience.

Strood

Listed as Strod in 889, this comes from Old English *strod* and describes 'the marshy land overgrown with brushwood'.

Barnfield is a fairly common name in the county, seen at least five times and always from *bern feld* 'the open land with or by a barn'. What began as a description of 'a wood beyond the barn' is today seen as Head Barn Wood. Ranscombe is found as Rainescumbe in 1199 and Rennescumbe in 1203, the name from Old English *hraefnes cumb* and speaking of 'the valley frequented by ravens'. Rede Court is found as Rede in 1270, this is from *ried* and speaks of 'the land cleared of trees and undergrowth'.

Stogarts and Drapers Wood effectively refers to two names for the same place. The first is from *stocc geat* or 'the gate made of stumps', while the second is a reminder of a family called Draper, here before 1698, the earliest record of this name. A minor place name, now used for the local pub, is the Three Crutches. In 1695 this was Three Crouches, showing this was from Middle English *crouche* or 'cross'. Wicham Cottages derive their name from *wicham* and quite simply means 'dwelling place'. Merrals Shaw is the modern version of what began as Mirralds Ground and Mirralds Wood. No records of this name are found before 1698 and hence there is no link to a landholder or family of this name but there is no other plausible explanation.

The Bounty is a pub name of obvious origins for the street named outside is Bligh Street. Put the two together and the word 'mutiny' comes to mind. Two centuries later and arguments as to whether the mutiny was justifiable or not show the answer will probably never be known, although his reputation as a hard task master and strict disciplinarian are supported by those who incurred his wrath at other times in his life. Interestingly the name was popular before Fletcher Christian led the mutiny, however then it was used quite differently to mean 'generosity'.

Two soldiers who fought at Agincourt on 25 October 1415 are reputed to have opened and named the Crispin and Crispianus pub at Strood. The link being that date is the feast day of St Crispin, with Crispianus being the name of his brother.

Sundridge

The Domesday survey lists this name as Sondresse, showing this to be from Old English *sundor ersc* and describing 'the separate or detached ploughed field'.

Burford is first recorded in 1616, although the name is from the much earlier Old English *burh ford* and refers to 'the stronghold by a ford'. Combebank Farm is easy to see as 'the bank of land in or near the valley'.

Sutton at Hone

The basic name here is one of the most common in the country, always from Old English *suth tun* and meaning it was 'the southern farmstead', that is south of that which named it so. Listed as Sudtone in 1086 and as Sutton atte Hone in 1240, the addition here is derived from *han* 'the boundary stone'.

Minor names begin with Gilden Hill, from Old English *gylden hyll* and telling of 'the golden hill', undoubtedly for the profusion of yellow flowers which grew here many years before the name was first recorded as Gyldenhill in 1406. St John's reminds us this manor was granted to the Knights Hospitallers if St John of Jerusalem by King John.

Sutton Valence

As if to prove the name of Sutton is a common one, here is a second example. Again this comes from old English *suth tun* and refers to 'the southern farmstead'. Here the addition is manorial, a reminder of the Valence family who were granted this manor by Henry III in 1265 – William de Valence being the king's own brother. The manor then passed to Amaury de Montfort, his son, and then to the Hastings family when the place was recorded as Sutton Hastings for a time. Having defined Sutton as 'the southern farmstead' it seems ludicrous to find a place called East Sutton. However it does make sense as it refers to it being east of the main place.

Nearby is the hamlet of Forsham, a name from Old English *forst hamm* and, recorded as Fforsthamme in 1261, describes 'the frosty water meadow'. This is an odd place name as the very origin of a name is to describe a place, to make it recognisable. Clearly days without frost greatly exceed those with, even in the worst winters. Hence this name may be carrying a different message, perhaps used the same as in 'a frosty reception' ie not welcoming. If so then this place is described as being difficult to build on or to farm. Lake Farm has no lake, at least not one which has given a name to the place. It does have a small stream, a tributary of the River Beult, and would have been a *lacu* to the Saxons. This term means simply 'watercourse'.

The Plough Inn has one of the most common pub names in the country. It came to prominence in the sixteenth century when almost everyone earned their living off the land and offers an invitation to those workers to drink within. The Cloth Makers Arms features an heraldic image seen since the sixteenth century.

Swanley

Found in a document from 1203 as Swanleg, there is no doubt this comes from Old English *swan leah* and refers to 'the woodland clearing of the herdsmen'.

Swanley's unusual welcome sign

To the south is Crockenhill, from Old English *crocc aern* or 'the slope with a crock house (a pottery)' and first seen in 1388 as Crokornheld. Hextable is found as Hagestapel and Heghstaple in the twelfth and thirteenth centuries, this from Old English *heah stapol* and telling this was 'the high post'. Whatever this *stapol* or 'post' marked is long forgotten.

Hockenden is found from the thirteenth century, this an Old English name referring to 'the woodland pasture of a man called Hoc'. Goss Hill is seen as Gorsindon in 1195 and as Gostendon in 1385, the name from *gorsten dun* or 'the hill covered with gorse'. Wested is a later place name, from Middle English *west stede* it describes 'the western place'.

Pubs start with the Fruiterers Arms, a name which links all those using not only fruit but also vegetables, these making an excellent sign as they are simple, attractive and instantly recognised.

Swanscombe

Records of this name include Suanescamp in 695 and as Svinescamp in 1086, a name from Old English *swan camp* and referring to 'the enclosed land of the herdsman'.

Alkerden Manor takes a local name which is not seen before 1778, prior to this it was recorded as Combe clearly *cumb* or 'valley'. However this is nothing like Alkerden which, despite the lack of records, is clearly from the Saxon era and probably represents the original name in describing 'the woodland pasture of a man called Ealhheard'. The suffix of Blendon is Old English *dun* and gives 'the hill of a man called Blaeda'.

Craylands takes the name from the family of Walter Greylaund, here in 1292. Galley Hill is a reminder of the late thirteenth century, when Robert Galyan is recorded as living at Swanescampe. Ingress Abbey was owned by the Priory of Dartford, the name showing this was 'an entrance place', ie where novices were trained. Stonewood tells us exactly what it is, the 'wood with stony ground'.

Excavations in the 1930s uncovered some skull bones of a human who lived here 400,000 years ago. Indeed so old and minimal are the remains it is impossible to tell if this represents the remains of early man in *Homo Sapiens* or a late example of *Homo Erectus*. Always referred to as Swanscombe Man and said to be the earliest evidence of man in Britain, the figure is now thought to be female and younger than the more primitive human discovered lower down and labelled Clactonian Man.

Sydenham

First recorded in 1206 where it appears as Chipeham, this is 'the homestead of a man called Clippa', where the Saxon personal name is suffixed by *ham*.

Cobbs Corner is a local name recalling the draper's shop run by Walter Cobb. This later grew to become a large department store but has retained its local name.

CHAPTER EIGHTEEN – T

Teise, River

A river named from a place name, a process known as backformation. Seen as Theise Hirst in 1577, the place is now known as Ticehurst. As the element *hyrst* or 'wooded hill' is absent from the river name we can ignore it, which leaves the first part meaning 'young goats'.

Teston

Listed in a tenth-century document as Terstan and as Testan in Domesday, this name comes from Old English *taer stan* and describes 'the stone with a gap or hole'.

Courtlands is derived from Middle English *curt tones land*, 'the farmstead at the short piece of land'.

Thames, River

An ancient river name and one where the earliest record of Tamesis from bc51 is one of the oldest known for any English place name. Indeed, so old is this name it is not clear if the meaning is 'the dark one' or simply 'river', although both allude to moving water.

Thamesmead

A very recent name and one created to refer to the new development alongside England's longest river.

Thong

Listed as Thuange at the end of the eleventh century, this name comes from Old English *thwang* and describes 'the narrow strip of land'.

Tonbridge

A name from Old English *tun brycg*, there can be no doubt this comes from 'the bridge of the farmstead'. The earliest surviving record is from Domesday in 1086, where the name appears as Tonebrige.

Barden Park takes its basic name from 'the *denn* or woodland pasture of a man called Baere', the name found as Barindena around the end of the eleventh century. Cage Farm is recorded as le Cagegate in 1483 and as Cage in 1533, which can only mean the farm followed the site of a 'cage on the way' where minor criminals were once held. Hectorage Farm was found as Le Hethehirts in 1292, from *haeth hyrst* or 'where heather grows on a wooded hill'. Trench is self-explanatory and does describe this lane as having 'a ditch'.

Capel is a Middle English word for 'chapel', the place name recorded since the thirteenth century. Crockhurst Street is derived from the Celtic term *cruc* with Old English *hyrst* telling of 'the wooded hill', street being a much later addition. Gregg's Wood can be traced to the family of Robert Grigge, the first of his line to be documented and here in 1347. Haysden is recorded as Hesdenn in 1232, from *haes denn* this is 'the woodland pasture overgrown with brushwood'. Hawden is first seen in the record from 1301 as Hauedenne from the suffix *denn* and a Saxon personal name telling us it was 'the woodland pasture of a man called Haefa'.

Holden comes from Old English *hol denn* and describes 'the woodland pasture in a hollow'. Postern Lane and Postern Park Farm share a name originating in Old French *posterne* saying this was the 'back or side entrance'. Putland's took the name of the family who were associated with this place in the early eighteenth century. Southfrith Lodge exists as 'the southern woodland', Old English *suth fyrhthe* recorded as Sutfrith in 1295 and as Southfrith for the first time in 1610. Stone Bridge is self-explanatory, the name remaining largely unchanged since it was first seen in 1334.

Pub signs are advertisements, invitations to enter and partake of what is on offer. Trades are a popular subject, although often difficult to understand whether it is relevant to the landlord's former occupation or one prevalent in the region. It seems more likely the former is true in the case of the Carpenters Arms. In the Blue Bell Inn we see an indication this was associated with the local church, who probably held the land here. The bell is a common indicator of the church, whilst the colour is always a pointer to Christianity.

In the Half Moon we see a name which is often depicted as one phase of the moon, sometimes waxing and others when it is waning. However it came to be a pub name from an heraldic symbol, where the moon shape is shown as a crescent lying on its back with the 'horns' pointing upwards. This was used to show the family's ancestors had fought in the Crusades to the Holy Land. Another military figure is shown outside the Kentish Rifleman, although the member of the Home Guard shown is unlikely to be the true origin but dates from much earlier when those who wished to serve in the army outside of any recruitment drive were required to purchase their own weapon and pay to for the lessons before they were allowed to join up. The military theme continues in the Gun and Spitroast, known simply as the Gun until the 1930s when an adjoining restaurant suggested its own addition.

At the Humphrey Bean we find a pub named after a former landlord of the pub which stood on this site at the beginning of the twentieth century known as the We Three Loggerheads. The riverside location suggested itself at the Wharf. The Stags Head is ultimately a reminder of the days of the royal hunt, whether this be directly or through a device from a coat of arms is difficult to say. No difficulty in the name of the Punch and Judy, this traditional puppet show was brought to our shores in the seventeenth century but has not always been the sole enjoyment of children. The children of Tonbridge suffered because of the failure of Cardinal Wolsey to deliver his promised grammar school to the town. Hence the name of the Cardinal's Error public house although, to be fair, it was hardly his fault he lost and job and died shortly afterwards.

Trottiscliffe

Whether we examine the record of Trottes clyva in 788 or Domesday's Totesclive, it is difficult to be certain of the personal name here. However the suffix is certainly Old English *clif*, together this gives 'the cliff or bank of a man called Tortt'.

Westpark Farm tells us this was 'the estate west of the parish'.

Tudeley

Listed as Tivedele in Domesday, this name is derived from Old English *ifede leah* and describes 'the woodland clearing overgrown with ivy'. That this has acquired an initial 'T' is quite commonplace for a name beginning with a vowel, Middle English *atte* or 'at' preceded this name and the final 'T' migrated from 'at' to the beginning of the following word. Sherenden is from Old English *scearn denn*, the 'woodland pasture where dung is collected' is recorded from the thirteenth century.

Tunbridge Wells

Despite the change in spelling this certainly has been transferred here from the name of Tonbridge, with the addition of the medicinal springs exploited here since the seventeenth century. Often heard as Royal Tunbridge Wells, this was bestowed upon the town following the visit of Edward VII.

Royal Tunbridge Wells sign with

....

138

..... an inset of the coat of arms.

Bayhall Road features an old place names from *beg halh* 'the corner of land where prickly shrubs grow'. The record of 1292 as Bishoppesdoun show the modern name of Bishop's Down refers to 'the *dun* or hill of the family of Bisshop', one Robert Bisshop was here in 1352 and Joan Bishoppe in 1514. Broadmead has existed since at least the thirteenth century, from *brad maed* this is 'the broad meadow'. A reminder of the occupancy of Thomas Hogge is seen in Hoggs Bridge, here crossing a stream, a tributary of the Beult. Early listings of Kingsland as Cyninges Folcland in 858 show this to be from *cyninges folc land* or 'the folk land of the king'.

Hawkenbury is one of two places of this name in Kent, although the other in Headcorn in West Kent has a different meaning. This example is recorded as Hokyngbury in 1258, where a Saxon personal name precedes *inga burh* and describes 'the stronghold of the family or followers of a man called Hoc'. Mouseden has nothing to do with rodents but comes from *meos denn* or 'the woodland pasture where moss is found'. Pinkhorn Green features a Saxon personal name with Old English *hruna* and speaks of 'the fallen trees of a man called Pineca'.

Wybournes is a place showing it was associated with the family of Robert and Roger Wybarn in the fourteenth century. Historically recorded as Heselette, and similar, since the early fourteenth century and speaking of 'the copse of hazel trees', the modern version of Hazelpits must be derived from this but the change in suffix is a mystery. Lamberts Land has been seen since the fourteenth century, a name which can be attributed to the family first recorded as belonging to Adam Lambert in 1259.

Normally place names ending in –hall are derived from *halh* or 'nook of land', very rarely does this represent 'hall' in the modern sense. However looking at the earliest records of Rusthall we find this was originally

Rustuwelle, literally 'the rusty spring' and from *rust wielle* it refers to the colour of the water from springs in the area as a result of the minerals therein. Then in the thirteenth century a building or hall was erected here which was misinterpreted as the origin of the name and thereafter the place became Rusthall. Dornden is found as Thorndenn in 1292, this from Old English *thorn denn* and describing 'the woodland pasture with many thornbushes'.

Pippins derives its name from the family of Richard Pyppyn, here by 1346. Ramslye appears as Ramesleye in 1271, this being from *hraefnes leah* or 'the woodland clearing frequented by ravens'. Smockham Farm is an interesting name as it describes, very specifically, the activities in Saxon times. Found as Smocham in 1191, this represents *smock ham* or 'the homestead where smocks are made'. Boarden is seen as Burdenn in 1254, this from Old English *burna denn* or 'the woodland pasture at a stream'. Great Culverden is derived from Old English *culfre denn* or 'the woodland pasture frequented by doves'.

Local pub names begin with the Nevill Crest and Gun, one of the pubs which has acquired its name through the amalgamation of two former pub names. In the Nevill Crest is the image associated with the Nevill family, marquesses of Abergavenny, who have their family seat here. In the case of the Gun the name was transferred here when one licence was issued to cover both places under one landlord.

At the Duke of York Ale House the name refers to the title granted to the second son of the monarch on the occasion of his marriage. It is also the title of a nursery rhyme, a ditty telling of Prince Frederick Augustus, son of George III and his command of the British forces in Flanders. However it is quite inaccurate in its description for he did not command ten thousand men but over three times that number, marched them up nor down a gradient for there are no hills in this part of the world, and while he may have been grand he certainly was not 'old' for he was just 31 when he returned home.

The Pitcher and Piano is not only an example of alliteration but links together two seemingly unrelated objects, thus making it the perfect pub name. In effect the two are linked, the pitcher being filled with ale which in turn filled the glasses of those gathered around the piano for a good old sing-song. Hence a good time was had by all. A building once housing the

Romary Biscuit Factory, founded by Alfred Romary in 1862, and is now a public house named, appropriately enough, the Biscuit Factory.

At the Kentish Yeoman the name refers to the soldier, initially a volunteer cavalryman. At the Mitre is a sign using the image of the hat worn by a bishop, clearly a link to the church. The Crystal Palace was named after the magnificent building, constructed mainly from glass, which housed the Great Exhibition of 1851. The Abergavenny Arms was named after Lord Abergavenny, who owned this land until 1933. Nineteenth century brewer Edward Kelsey is remembered in the Kelsey Arms. Richard Nash had a reputation as a dandy and a gambler, which tended to detract from his skills as a manager, he was known by the nickname which adorns the pub called the Beau Nash.

A man who surely should have more pubs named after him is Sir Alf Ramsey, manager of the England football team when they won the Jules Rimet Trophy (or the World Cup) in 1966. His playing career was restricted to two clubs, Southampton and Tottenham Hotspur, while prior to the England job he managed Ipswich Town and after England he filled in for six months at Birmingham City. Another sport gave a name to the Long Bow, local woman Mrs Nettleton a world champion archer in the 1930s.

CHAPTER NINETEEN – U

Ulcombe

Records of this name begin in 946 as Ulancumbe, with the later Olecumbe in the Domesday survey of 1086. This comes from Old English *ule cumb* and describes 'the valley of the owls'.

Boy Court is a Middle English name, from *boian cot* this is 'the cottage of the young men', similarly Boyton Court refers to 'the farmstead of the young men'. Kingsnoad comes from Old English *cyninges snad* to describe 'the detached land of the king'. Marshall Wood took its name from John Marchal, a resident who is recorded here before 1332. Roselands Farm took its name from the family of William Rose, here in 1461.

Underriver

Listed for the first time in 1477, where the name is seen as Sub le Ryver. However this name is not exactly what it seems for this is no underwater location but comes from Old English *under yfer* and describes the place 'below the brow of the hill'.

Black Charles is a house, one which takes the name of former residents the Blakecherl or Blaccheri family, depending upon whether the thirteenth or fourteenth century records are the more accurate. Fawke Common and Fawke Farm are reminders of the family of Richard le Ffalke, recorded here by 1327. Great Hollanden is from *holegn denn* or 'the woodland pasture where holly grows', clearly there was once another of this name nearby for the addition of 'Great'.

In defining the name of the White Rock public house, we likely discover a link to Wales. Here the Welsh folksong *David of the White Rock* points to an early landlord being from the principality.

CHAPTER TWENTY – V

Vigo

A modern place name and one which is said to commemorate the capture of the Spanish port of Vigo by the British in 1719. The local pub follows this trend in being named the Villager.

To the north-east is Fairseat, a comparatively modern name from the late eighteenth century telling of the pleasant view.

CHAPTER TWENTY ONE – W

Wainscott

No early forms have survived through the years, yet it seems impossible this does not have Old English beginnings. This almost certainly comes from *waegnes cot* and tells of 'the cottages where wagons are kept'. This is among the author's favourite names as simply by defining it this draws a mental image of the place during Saxon times, something no artist would record and no camera could.

Walderslade

From Old English *weald slaed* comes a name meaning 'the valley in the forest' which was recorded as Waldeslade in 1190.

To the north Snodhurst Wood gets its name from Old English *snad hyrst* and tells us it was 'the wooded hill by a detached piece of land'. Cossington is recorded from the tenth century, where a Saxon personal name is followed by *ing tun* to tell of 'the farmstead associated with a man called Cusa'.

Wateringbury

A name meaning 'the stronghold of the family or followers of a man called Ahthere', this comes from a Saxon or Jute personal name and Old English *inga burh*. We find records of this place as Uuotryngebyri in 964 and as Otringeberge in 1086.

Canon Court, Great Canon and Little Canon share an origin reminding us this was the property of the prior and canons of Leeds during the reign of Henry III. Danns Lane was associated with the Dan family, known to have been in nearby Mereworth at the end of the fifteenth century. Pizien Well refers to a small stream once acting as an open sewer, if there was any doubt the record from 1473 of Pyssyngwelle makes it clear. Red Hill is self-explanatory, the reference is to the colour of the soil.

When it comes to pub names the Railway is not surprisingly named for that mode of transport, an advertisement to travellers and showing their hospitality was on offer. However it does serve to date the pub as it clearly cannot have been named before the trains arrived.

Watling Street

One of the four major roads covered by William the Conqueror's laws promising safe passage for travellers. This very political gesture was the reason the name has been transferred to others throughout England, although there is no physical connection between them. This is a Roman road, roughly following the line of the modern A5 trunk road between Dover and Holyhead off Anglesey, although the Roman part only reached Wroxeter.

Listed as Waetlinga straet in 880, Waeclinga straet in 926, and Watlingan straet in 957, this name can be traced back to one very small stretch of this 240 mile road. That small part was around the place name recorded as Waecelingaceaster around the end of the ninth century, a name meaning 'the Roman station of the people of Wacol', an old name for what is now known as St Albans.

Weald

A more common name than we would think, although most often seen in combination with a second element. This represented Old English *weald* and refers to 'the woodland'. The name is recorded as Waldum in 1185.

Bowzell comes from Old English *boc selle*, a description of 'a building by the beech tree'.

Welling

Listed as Wellynges in 1362, this name probably refers to this as 'the place of the springs', although the records are quite late and there was a family called Welling, here by the fourteenth century, who may have brought the name with them. What is certain is the long-standing local explanation for the place name as being from the days when horsepower meant just that and, having travelled from London, to reach here meant one was 'well in" to Kent.

Bethel Row, seen today as Bethel Road, can be traced back to 1327 and the family called Betyl who are still here in 1348 when seen as Betil. Clearly the original meaning was to a 'row' or line of dwellings.

The local pub is the Lord Kitchener, a British field marshal and statesman whose face on the recruiting posters during the First World War pointing out "Your Country Needs You" is probably the reason his face is better known than his name today. Another is the Foresters Arms, named for it being a meeting place or lodge of the Ancient Order of Foresters, a friendly society with branches across the United Kingdom and the United States of America.

We Anchor In Hope is a slightly different version of the more usual pub name of Hope and Anchor. However the meaning is the same. It is a reference to the Book of Hebrews in the Bible where St Paul speaks of one's faith being the anchor through life's storms and thus a religious name. Taken from the name of the hero featured in the eighteenth century work *Reliques*, the name of Guy Earl of Warwick has been written about since the twelfth century.

Westerham

Domesday lists this name as Oistreham in 1086, with the earlier record of Westarham in 871. Here is 'the westerly homestead' from Old English *wester ham*.

Bardogs is a manorial name, John Bardog is seen here in 1450 while earlier, in 1313, the Bardehog family are represented by John, Nicholas and William. Betsom's Hill recalls the family of John Bettesham, recorded here for the first time in 1499. Chartwell is the name of the house built on the *cert wielle* or 'the spring on the rough common'. Force Green takes the name of Martin le Forst, recorded here in 1254. Grays Farm and Little Grays share an origin in the family who held this land, first recorded in 1284 in the name of William le Grey. Mariners remembers the family of William Maryner, here by 1382.

French Street remembers the family of John le Ffrenche, recorded as being here in a document dated 1332. The earliest surviving record of Gaysham dates from 1312 and is exactly as it appears today. Here the Old English *ham* follows a Saxon or Jute personal name and describes 'the homestead of a man called Gaeg'. Goodley Stock is recorded as Goldelegh in 1278, the early name coming from Old English *golde leah* and referring to 'the woodland clearing where marigolds abound'. It is important to realise a *leah* is a natural clearing, for the later addition of *stocc* refers to 'tree stumps'. Two possibilities here, either two separate places have grown and merged or the original site was extended.

Mapleton Lodge began as Napleton, the name coming from Old English *aet thaem aeppeltune* meaning 'at the orchard'. Thus the correct name should be atten-appletree-farmstead, where the final 'n' has migrated to the beginning of the name of the fruit. The modern form is a corruption. In the case of Uplands Farm the name means exactly what it seems, the 'upper agricultural land' first seen in a document from 1278. Valence is an old family name, that of De Valoniis or Valons seen in documents detailing landholders of Westerham in the thirteenth century. The earliest forms of Coakham appear in the thirteenth century as Cobbecumbe and Cobecumbe, these showing the modern name is a contraction of 'the *cumb* or valley of a man called Cobba'. A family name is seen in Pootens, the de Potone name first documented here in 1327.

On hearing someone say "George and Dragon", we instantly think of a pub name and not the patron saint of England and his most famous deed. This is down to the position of the definite article, 'the George and Dragon' is the pub and 'George and the Dragon' the patron saint, and yet when we hear these spoken it is doubtful if this subtle difference is ever noticed. A sign depicting a device found on the coat of arms of Sir Thomas Gresham, a sixteenth century merchant and financier, has given a name to the Grasshopper on the Green along with an indication of its location.

Westerham was the birthplace of James Wolfe, who led the British expeditionary forces against the French under Montcalm at the Heights of Abraham in Quebec, Canada. Both leaders were killed during the battle, with the local man remembered by the pub named the General Wolfe. There is a military link to the Old House At Home, this being a traditional ballad where a son dreams of his mother and the comfort of home. The close proximity of Biggin Hill and its association with the air is seen in the name of the Flying Machine.

West Kingsdown

Listed as Kingesdon in 1199, this name comes from Old English *cyning dun* and refers to 'the king's hill'. The addition is to distinguish this from Kingsdown near Deal.

Nearby is Brands Hatch, a name synonymous with motor racing for over fifty years. The circuit lies within a natural amphitheatre, making it ideal as a stadium for competitors and spectators alike. As a place name the earliest surviving record comes from 1292 as Bronkesesch, from Old English *brances haecc* 'the gate or gap on a slope or brink'. Hence by defining the name we are reminded of the topography which has made this place famous internationally.

Chimhams is from Middle English *chimbe ham* and describes 'the homestead near a projecting rim'. This hamlet standing on high ground is recorded as Chimbeham in 1203 and Chimbham in 1254. In 1313 it was recorded as La Knocke, from Old English *cnocc* meaning 'hillock' and seen on modern maps as Knockmill. Hence while the records show nothing of a mill here, there is no doubt there was once such here. Cowless Shaw may not have surviving records prior to 152 as Cowles, but the name is certainly much older for here is the Saxon or Old English *cu laes* 'the meadow where cows are grazed'. Hazelden can be traced back to 1256 as Hasilden, this from *haesel denn* and telling of 'the woodland pasture where hazels grow'.

The Portobello Inn is a pub named in honour of the most famous achievement of Admiral Edward Vernon. In 1739 he captured the

Panamanian port of Porto Bello from the Spaniards, even though his 'fleet' numbered just six ships. He also served several terms as a member of parliament. In the Gamecock, we find a pub named for the breed of cockerel used in cock-fighting and showing this was a venue for the 'sport' banned in the middle of the nineteenth century.

West Wickham

A basic name which is quite common, hence the need for the addition to distinguish it from others. Here the two common elements have slightly different meanings and thus should be seen as 'the homestead associated with the vicus of an earlier Romano-British settlement'.

Layham's Farm is a local name from *laege hamm*, 'the fallow hemmed in land'. Pickhurst literally means 'point wood' and is derived from *pic hyrst*, the point being the shape this topographical feature appeared to form to the observer. It has also given a name to Pickhurst Lane and the Pickhurst Arms.

Wigmore

A corruption of Old English *wid mere* which describes 'the broad pool', this name appears as Wydemere in 1275.

To the east is Meresborough, a name originally seen as simply Mere in 1197 and meaning 'pool'. The addition is much more recent and points to this being the meeting place for the local court. From Old English *mersc geat*, listed as Mersgate in 1270, comes Marshgate and literally describes 'the gateway to the marsh'. Note the Saxon use of *geat* refers to the path and not the barrier across it.

Wilmington

A Saxon or Jute personal name with Old English *ing tun* gives 'the farmstead associated with a man called Wighelm'. The name is recorded as Wilmintuna in 1089.

Minor names include Hulse Wood, named after Richard Hulse, an eighteenth century landowner in and around the Dartford area. Rowhill Wood, Rowhill Mount and Rowhill Grange share an origin in Old English *ruh hyll* 'the rough hill' and a name first seen in the early thirteenth century. Found as Heselwode in 1332, Old English *haesel wudu* or 'the wood of hazel trees' is seen as Hazelwood today.

Woolwich

The two earliest forms of this name seem to have little in common with the modern form. Domesday gives this as Hulviz in 1086, with the even stranger earlier form of Uuluuich in 918. Here the Old English elements *wull wic* refer to 'the port or harbour where wool is shipped'.

Wouldham

Here a Saxon or Jute personal name and Old English *ham* combine to tell of 'the homestead of a man called Wulda'.

Buckmore Wood is derived from Old English *bucca mere* 'the pool of the bucks'. The Watermans Arms, from the Worshipful Company of Watermen and Lightermen, is a pub name remembering a trade which involves working with boats and barges in any number of ways.

Wrotham

Recorded as Uurotaham in 788 and as Broteham in 1086, this comes from a Saxon or Jute personal name and Old English *ham* and speaks of 'the homestead of a man called Wrota'.

Child's Bridge is a local name, also seen in Childs Way, recorded as Chelde in 1280 and Childe in 1539, this comes from Old English *celde* or Middle English *chelde* and describes 'the sping', a reference to a tributary of the Darent. Coldharbour is a common place name, named so travellers would know it as a place of refuge in bad weather. It was probably a corruption of the original name for in the fourteenth century it was known as 'the field called Caldham', that place name describing 'the cold hemmed-in land'.

Crowhurst is a common English place name, from *crawe hyrst* it describes 'the wooded hill frequented by crows'. Nepicar House takes a minor place name first seen in 1292 and derived from *naep aecer* or 'the land where turnips are cultivated'. Phen Farm tells us it was worked by 'the dweller at the fen', for that is how the Venne family get their name. Terry's Lodge can be traced to the family of William and Thomas Terry, recorded here for the first time in 1452.

CHAPTER TWENTY TWO – Y

Yalding

Found as Hallinges in the Domesday record of 1086 and as Ealding in 1207, this comes from a Saxon or Jute personal name and Old English *ingas*. Together these speak of the '(place of) the family or followers of a man called Ealda'.

To the south Benover is from *ofer* with a Saxon personal name telling of 'the bank of a man called Bealde', this being the bank of the River Beult. Kenward comes directly from a surname, the family held land in this parish during the reign of Henry VIII. As a settlement Laddingford originally stood near where a ford crossed the River Teise, yet this was not the original name of the river. Here was the Lodena, a British or Celtic river name meaning 'the muddy one'. Clearly the modern place name describes 'the ford across the muddy one'.

As a street name Pikefish Lane is most unusual. For this to be derived from the freshwater predator *Esox Lucius* a extraordinary and unknown sequence of events must have occurred. More likely this began as a nickname and was passed down as a surname to a family who are recorded here in 1327 headed by Richard Pykeuys. Rugmore Hill is seen as Ruggeme in 1292, with 'the pool of a man called Rugga' featuring a Saxon personal name and Old English *mere*. Hampstead Lane is derived from Old English *ham stede* and refers to 'the homestead place', this name recorded as Hamsted in 1240 and as Hampstede in 1338.

Public houses include the George, this a reference to the patron saint of England, St George.

CHAPTER TWENTY THREE

Common Place-Name Elements

Element	Origin	Meaning
ac	Old English	oak tree
banke	Old Scandinavian	bank, hill slope
bearu	Old English	grove, wood
bekkr	Old Scandinavian	stream
berg	Old Scandinavian	hill
birce	Old English	birch tree
brad	Old English	broad
broc	Old English	brook, stream
brycg	Old English	bridge
burh	Old English	fortified place
burna	Old English	stream
by	Old Scandinavian	farmstead
ceap	Old English	market
ceaster	Old English	Roman stronghold
cirice	Old English	church
clif	Old English	cliff, slope
cocc	Old English	woodcock
cot	Old English	cottage
cumb	Old English	valley
cweorn	Old English	queen
cyning	Old English	king
dael	Old English	valley
dalr	Old Scandinavian	valley
denu	Old English	valley
draeg	Old English	portage

dun	Old English	hill
ea	Old English	river
east	Old English	east
ecg	Old English	edge
eg	Old English	island
eorl	Old English	nobleman
eowestre	Old English	fold for sheep
fald	Old English	animal enclosure
feld	Old English	open land
ford	Old English	river crossing
ful	Old English	foul, dirty
geard	Old English	yard
geat	Old English	gap, pass
haeg	Old English	enclosure
haeth	Old English	heath
haga	Old English	hedged enclosure
halh	Old English	nook of land
ham	Old English	homestead
hamm	Old English	river meadow
heah	Old English	high, chief
hlaw	Old English	tumulus, mound
hoh	Old English	hill spur
hop	Old English	enclosed valley
hrycg	Old English	ridge
hwaete	Old English	wheat
hwit	Old English	white
hyll	Old English	hill
lacu	Old English	stream, water course
lang	Old English	long
langr	Old Scandinavian	long
leah	Old English	woodland clearing
lytel	Old English	little
meos	Old English	moss
mere	Old English	lake

middel	Old English	middle
mor	Old English	moorland
myln	Old English	mill
niwe	Old English	new
north	Old English	north
ofer	Old English	bank, ridge
pol	Old English	pool, pond
preost	Old English	priest
ruh	Old English	rough
salh	Old English	willow
sceaga	Old English	small wood, copse
sceap	Old English	sheep
stan	Old English	stone, boundary stone
steinn	Old Scandinavian	stone, boundary stone
stapol	Old English	post, pillar
stoc	Old English	secondary or special settlement
stocc	Old English	stump, log
stow	Old English	assembly or holy place
straet	Old English	Roman road
suth	Old English	south
thorp	Old Scandinavian	outlying farmstead
treow	Old English	tree, post
tun	Old English	farmstead
wald	Old English	woodland, forest
wella	Old English	spring, stream
west	Old English	west
wic	Old English	specialised, usually dairy farm
withig	Old English	willow tree
worth	Old English	an enclosure
wudu	Old English	wood

CHAPTER TWENTY FOUR

Oxford Dictionary of English Place Names by A.D. Mills
The Concise Oxford Dictionary of English Place-Names by Eilert Ekwall
A Dictionary of Pub Names by Leslie Dunkling and Gordon Wright
The Place Names of Kent by Judith Glover

4913092R00089

Printed in Great Britain
by Amazon.co.uk, Ltd.,
Marston Gate.